Saint John Vianney

**The Village Priest
Who Fought God's Battles**

Saint John Vianney

The Village Priest
Who Fought God's Battles

by Leon Cristiani

Translated from the French
by M. Angeline Bouchard

ST. PAUL BOOKS & MEDIA

Imprimatur: ✠Humberto Cardinal Medeiros
Archbishop of Boston

Original French title: *Saint J.-Marie Vianney*
Nihil Obstat: Jean Gautier, Pss
Imprimatur: Michel Potevin, v.g.

Cover/Photo Credits: slide program: *Jean-Marie Vianney Prêtre,* Sonimages, 3 rue Amyot, 75005 Paris

Library of Congress Cataloging-in-Publication Data

Cristiani, Leon, 1987-
      The village priest who fought God's battles, Saint John Mary Vianney (1786-1859).
      Translation of Saint J.-Marie Vianney, curé d'Ars (1786-1859).
      1. Vianney, Jean Baptiste Marie, Saint, 1786-1859.
2. Christian saints—France—Ars (Ain)—Biography. 3. Ars, France (Ain)—Biography. I. Title
BX4700.V5C6613   282'.092'4 [B]   77-9339

Original English Title: *The Village Priest Who Fought God's Battles*

Second edition: 1994

Published by Pauline Books & Media, 50 St. Paul's Avenue, Boston, MA 02130

Pauline Books & Media is the publishing house of the Daughters of St. Paul, an international congregation of women religious serving the Church with the communications media.

Contents

Preface

This delightful book gives us many useful insights into the life and the experiences of St. John Vianney, who is certainly a saint for our times. He is a wonderful example of the love of God working in one of His chosen vessels in a very powerful way. One indication of his success in influencing people to give up their sinful ways and to accept the way of Christ was the fact that he was attacked so viciously by the devil.

This book shows us that the Lord blessed this humble French priest with an abundance of His charismatic gifts.

What the world is hungering for today is another St. John Vianney, a man of deep prayer, intense mortification and generous care for others; this was manifested by his unselfish ministering to all the thousands who flocked to the little village of Ars.

Pope John XXIII, who made a pilgrimage to Ars a few months after becoming a priest, wrote a beautiful encyclical letter about St. John Vianney. In it, Pope John stated that he himself was inspired by the Curé of Ars, and he held him up as a model for our day. In the Church today many others are coming to realize the values of the qualities that St. John Vianney exemplified in such a simple, inspiring way—his love of the poor, his spirit of unselfishness, his great love of the Eucharist and his awareness of the seriousness of sin.

May this book inspire all who read it to be filled with the spirit of this saint, a spirit of generous, unselfish Christian love.

Daniel Sheehan, C.P.M.

John Mary Vianney's Boyhood and Youth

Ars, a Village Blessed

In our world where distances have almost been conquered, where means of transportation have become so plentiful and rapid, it is ·easy for visitors, tourists and pilgrims to flock to France from many lands. Naturally, Catholic pilgrims take a special interest in the sacred shrines renowned for apparitions of our Lord and the Blessed Virgin Mary, among them Paray-le-Monial, Lourdes, La Salette and Pontmain. Then there are shrines which commemorate the lives of certain French saints. For instance, Lisieux honors St. Thérèse of the Child Jesus, the little Carmelite nun who became the patroness of the world's missions. Ars draws admirers of St. John Mary Vianney, the wonder-working village pastor who was named patron of all Catholic diocesan priests.

Ars is a tiny village in the Dombes region of eastern France between the Rhône and the Saône Rivers. It is a quiet, outwardly unchanging com-

11

munity spread out over a few hills that slope down toward Fontblin Creek, which flows into the Formans River. The simple homes of the town are clustered around a basilica with Byzantine cupolas, and a small, unassuming country church stands nearby. What do people come here to see?

What draws prayerful men and women to this spot? It is not the landscape, charming as it may be, or the majesty of some great monument. The magnet that attracts so many is the memory of a man, a priest who became a saint.

All the glory of Ars comes to it from this one man, this priest, better known as "the Curé of Ars" than by his own name John Mary Vianney.

In his life at Ars we shall see him in action, performing miracles, suffering and ministering to the needs of souls. There we shall witness what we might call his daily "martyrdom." He was the pastor of Ars for forty-one years, from 1818 to 1859. This was the only parish he ever had in his entire life. Ars is still filled with him. He is the one everyone comes to see, and it is at his feet that the thoughtful come to meditate and pray.

However, in this first chapter of our story, we want to call to mind his family background and early years, and watch him grow to manhood.

A Son of Old France

John Mary Vianney was a son of "Old France," the France that preceded the Revolution. It was a France not yet ravaged, shamed, and disfigured by violence and godlessness, a land that still preserved deep in its national consciousness the spirit of faith and charity conferred upon it by sixteen centuries of Christianity. The families of that day resembled those still to be found here and there in French Canada, where the magnificent traditions of Old France have been preserved.

John Mary Vianney was the fourth son of Matthew Vianney and Mary Beluse. Two daughters and a son had preceded him in the family. After him, another daughter and son were to be born. The Vianney family was outstanding for its practice of charity. They lived in the village of Dardilly, eight kilometers (4.96 miles) northwest of Lyons. All the beggars who plied the highroad in that area knew where they lived. Legends sprang up about the Vianneys like those of the Middle Ages. It was said that Jesus sometimes stood unnoticed among their forlorn visitors. One day, a saint was among their transient guests. This was St. Benedict Joseph Labre, the "beggar-saint" and a hero of prayer and penance. He passed that way in 1770, sixteen years before John Mary was born. His grateful prayers for the warm welcome he had received in this Christian home may have had a part in the raising up of another hero of prayer and penance like himself.

Prayer

In the traditional prayer in honor of the feast of John Mary Vianney, the liturgy praises him for three things: the intensity of his pastoral zeal, his constant prayer, and his unremitting penance. Now, the first thing that was noticed about him as a small child was his love of prayer. He really inherited this gift but it was nurtured by his devout mother. It was she who first taught him to make the Sign of the Cross, and made him repeat the deeply meaningful and charming words of the Lord's Prayer, the Hail Mary, and the Creed: *Our Father, who art in heaven!... Hail Mary, full of grace.... I believe in God, the Father Almighty....*

First Love

John Mary was the most docile, amiable, and intelligent of the Vianney children. By a mystery of Providence, he had inherited a greater abundance of the ancestral virtues from his father and mother. His spiritual precocity was soon apparent. He was scarcely four years old when some of its depth first appeared. He had received a lovely rosary which he cherished above everything else. Now, his younger sister Margaret, eighteen months his junior, tried to snatch it away from him. He protested. A childish battle ensued. Their mother separated them and said to John: "Son, give your rosary to Gothon.... Yes, give it to her for the love of God."

Without hesitation, and crying all the while, John Mary obeyed. This sacrifice was immediately rewarded. His mother immediately gave him a pretty wooden statuette of the Virgin Mary. His joy knew no bounds.

Nearly seventy years later, the Curé of Ars reminisced: "How I loved that little statue! I could not be separated from it day or night, and I would not have been able to sleep soundly if I had not had it by my side in my little bed.... The Blessed Virgin is my oldest love: I loved her even before I knew her...."

We cannot pass over this incident without stressing its importance. Here we find the tiny well-spring which would one day become a great river. The secret of the holiness of John Mary Vianney unquestionably lies in the power of his prayer. He began to pray as a small child, never to cease. The true story of any saint should be the story of his prayer. What the saints say to God and what God says to them explains everything about them. Unfortunately, it is this very personal and hidden story that no biographer is in a position to relate. It will be known to us only in heaven.

John Mary at Prayer

Even so, we can get some idea of John Mary as a child from his actions, his attitudes, and his naive stratagems. We almost always find him red-handed, so to speak, in the act of praying. If the *Angelus* rings, he is quick to fall to his knees before anyone else in the house. Sometimes, we catch a glimpse of him placing his precious little statue on a chair, and then kneeling he would pray before it. He learned from his mother to "bless" the chiming of every hour by reciting a *Hail Mary,* with a big Sign of the Cross before and after. Sometimes, he is heard to pray aloud, and the neighbors say to his mother:

"He knows lots of litanies. Your John Mary will become a priest or a brother."

One day, his mother searched for him everywhere and did not know what had become of him. She was terrified, because there was a large pond by the garden, where the cattle came to drink. She kept calling him, but received no answer. When she finally opened the stable door, what did she see close to the ruminating cows? Her child on his knees near the manger, praying fervently before his statuette of Mary. She took him up in her arms and said happily: "My little son, you were right there! Why do you hide like that to pray? You know we always pray together!"

One of John Mary's first joys was to accompany his mother to church. As often as she could, she went to daily Mass. As soon as the churchbells rang to announce Mass, John begged his mother to take him with her. She would explain the ceremonies of the Mass to him. Above all, he learned to pray by watching his mother at prayer before the altar. He was already falling in love with the tabernacle which would later be his divine torment, his sacred love. Happy the child, happy the man who can say what he said about his mother when he was being congratulated for having developed a love of prayer so early in life:

"After God, I owe it to my mother. She was so wise! Virtue passes easily from the hearts of mothers into the hearts of their children.... Everyone who has had the good fortune to have a saintly mother should weep [with joy] when he looks at her or thinks about her!..."

As John Mary grew up, his love of prayer grew apace. When he led the cattle to the fields, accompanied by his youngest sister, he never forgot to bring his precious statuette. Once in the meadow, situated in the hollow of a delightful valley known as *Chante-Merle,* which means "Sing-Blackbird," they would both kneel in prayer. Quickly going up to a hollow willow trunk, he would set the Madonna in it, adorn it with field flowers, and then begin to say his rosary. He loved to build little chapels, to model little statues out of the clay soil. Some of these statuettes were so well made that his father baked one of them in the oven, and kept it in the house a long while.

If other children came out into the field to tend their flocks, John Mary would quickly gather them into a group and preach childish sermons to them, imitating the pastor of his church, and then he would organize a procession. As he said later, "I was almost always the one who took the part of the pastor!"

A Land Without Priests

These little scenes may seem very childish indeed. But if we consider them in the context of the times, they take on a wealth of meaning. John Mary was just three years old when the States General convened in May, 1789. He was just three years old when earth-shaking events happened for France: the Oath of the *Jeu de Paume,* the capture of the Bastille, the night of August 4th, and the October Days. He was four years old when the Civil Constitution of the Clergy was voted. He was only five when the pastor of Dardilly, Father Jacques Rey, either mistakenly or out of weakness, pledged the oath of allegiance to this Constitution condemned by the Church, then retracted his pledge and withdrew to Lyons before going to Italy.

A priest who had accepted the Constitution came to Dardilly, one of those commonly referred to as a "juror," or a "juring priest." At first the Vianneys didn't quite understand what had happened. As soon as they fully realized what was at stake, they stopped attending the services at which this schismatic priest officiated. From that time on, they associated only with faithful priests who, at the peril of their life, came from time to time into the area to celebrate Mass secretly in a barn or perhaps in an attic.

The Vianneys were among the fervent Christians who agreed to harbor fugitive priests. The sacred liturgy was sometimes actually celebrated in their home. We can better appreciate the charm of John Vianney's improvised religious ceremonies out in the *Chante-Merle* meadow or elsewhere, when we remember the terrible events that were then unfolding throughout France.

This was a time when churches and cathedrals were being boarded up all over France. The statues and crosses erected at crossroads were being broken and torn down, priests were hunted men. Everywhere the abominable program to destroy religion was being put into effect. Amid all this devastation, the voice of a small boy could be heard preaching to other children, reciting the rosary with them, and holding processions which were forbidden by law. And so the torch of religious belief, instead of dying out, was passed from hand to hand, until it shone forth once more on the day willed by God with a new and more radiant light.

At School

Early in the year 1795, a teacher named Dumas opened a school in Dardilly. It attracted many pupils, among them little John Vianney, who was soon held up by his teacher as a model to his comrades. He quickly learned to read and write. When he returned home, he loved to read the *Lives of the Saints* aloud to the family, and to teach his sister Gothen her catechism. John Mary attended the school of Citizen Dumas for three years. But in May, 1798, a significant change occurred in his life.

First Confession, First Communion

In spite of the threatening prohibitions by the Revolutionary authorities, religious worship was reorganized in the Diocese of Lyons. A noted historian, Charles Ledré, has told about it in a beautiful book entitled *Le Culte caché sous la Révolution: Les Missions de l'Abbé Linsolas.*[1] The entire diocese was divided into apostolic sectors. Priests, disguised as artisans of all kinds, secretly served the parishes. Ecully, which was not far from Dardilly, had become one of the mission centers from which four priests exercised their heroic ministry in all the surrounding towns and villages. One of these priests was Father Groboz, who passed for a master cook. He happened to come to Dardilly and entered the Vianney's home. After blessing the children, he turned to John Mary who attracted him with his candid manner.

"How old are you?" the priest asked.
"Eleven, Sir."
"How long is it since you went to confession?"
"I've never been to confession!"
"Well then, let's get to it right away."

---

1. (Secret Religious Worship under the Revolution: The Missions of Father Linsolas.)

And right then and there John Vianney made his first confession. Later on, he recalled: "I still remember it very well. It was at our house, right in front of the big clock."

Before leaving, the priest urged the family to send the boy to Ecully to be given catechism lessons by two ladies, so he could prepare for his First Communion.

As it happened, his mother's sister, Mme. Humbert, lived in Ecully, and he was sent to live with her and her family. There were two nuns in lay attire at Ecully preparing a group of fifteen children for their First Holy Communion. John's new companions soon learned to admire his love of prayer. The spiritual wellspring was still growing in his soul. To quote Msgr. Trochu, one of the best historians of the Curé of Ars, "He prayed and prayed. He really didn't enjoy anything else." One witness has related: "Already at that young age, we thought of him as a little saint." Actually, his comrades sometimes teased him: "Look at the little fat boy," they would say, "wrestling with his guardian angel!"

John Mary Vianney made his First Communion when he was thirteen, during the haying season of 1799. The ceremony took place in Mme. de Pingon's parlor at Ecully. All the shutters had been shut tight. Outside the windows of the parlor several workmen busily unloaded large hay wagons. Inside, two nonjuring priests, Fathers Grobos and Balley, carried out their magnificent ministry before a tearful audience.

Years later, Marguerite Vianney, whom we already know as little Gothon, said: "My brother was so happy; he didn't want to leave the room where he had had the joy of receiving Communion for the first time."

Very probably, he had prolonged his thanksgiving after Communion so long that everyone thought he didn't want to leave.

This is a good place to recall what John Mary said about Communion in later years:

"When we receive Communion, we sense something extraordinary...a great joy,... a consolation..., a well-being that permeates our whole being and makes us tremble.... We cannot but say with St. John, 'It is the Lord!' O my God! What joy for a Christian to get up from the sacred banquet and go forth with all of heaven in his heart!"

Fifty years after that autumn day in 1799, he proudly showed to the children of Ars the plain rosary he had carried around his arm on the day of his First Communion. He still could not speak of that day without tears.

Dawn Breaks

Was it on the day of his First Communion that John Mary Vianney first thought of becoming a priest? There is no way to know for sure. And yet the great fervor of love of God he then experienced was the dawn of his apostolic career.

A dawn of another sort would soon break over the Catholic Church in France. During that same year, 1799, the coup d'état of 18 Brumaire (September 18th) overthrew the Directorate and brought to power a young Corsican general with a powerful and dominating personality. He did not hesitate to restore religious peace to the country and to enter into negotiations with Pope Pius VII to give France a new religious statute.

Against the opposition of all factions of his entourage consisting of Jacobins and atheists, Napoleon Bonaparte, the First Consul, signed the famous Convention of the Concordat on July 16, 1801. After it was ratified by the national legislature on April 5, 1802, this Concordat became effective as of April 18, 1802.

The churches of France were reopened. Everywhere church bells rang out once more. Father Jacques Rey returned from exile to his duties as pastor of Dardilly.

No one was so happy over these events as John Mary Vianney. His love of prayer had never ceased growing. During the intervening years from 1799 to 1802 he had worked with his father and older brother, plowing the fields and tending the vineyard by their side. Here too, he had continued to pray amidst his labors. Often he found he was not able to keep pace with his older brother in the vineyard. Then he would devoutly kiss his little statue of the Virgin Mary, set it down at some distance in front of him, and work as hard as he could until he had caught up with the older boy. Once again, he'd kiss the statue, set it down ahead of him, and start anew. So it went until evening. Back at the house, he could say to his mother proudly:

"Always put your trust in the Blessed Virgin Mary. I prayed hard to her today and she helped me. I was able to keep up with Francis, and I wasn't tired!"

During the year 1802 the thought of becoming a priest became more pressing. Speaking to his mother and also to his aunt, Mme. Humbert, he would say: "If I were a priest, I would want to win many souls!"

On the face of it, the very idea was ridiculous. He was sixteen years old, and had only an elementary-school education. He would need to learn Latin, a terrifying task for a country lad like John Vianney! Besides, where could he go to learn this ancient language? To whom could he turn for help?

The voice kept making itself heard deep within him. He could no longer silence it. He yearned to become a priest, to stand at the altar, to save souls. Could there be a nobler goal? When he finally spoke to his mother about it, she wept for joy. However, when he broached the matter to his father, he was roughly and definitively rebuffed.

A Providential Teacher

During the year 1803 it was learned that one of the priests who had been present at John's First Communion, Father Charles Balley, had been named pastor of Ecully. Formerly a religious, he was a learned and a devout man. Under his austere exterior, he was known to be very kind. This was the man Providence chose to prepare the heart of a saint. His success in this undertaking was enough to make him a great man in his own right.

One of Father Balley's first concerns upon coming to Ecully was to recruit vocations to the priesthood. He had opened a small school in his rectory for this purpose. There were soon two or three children studying under his guidance. When John Mary heard about this, he was elated. He begged his mother to find a way to overcome his father's disapproval. She agreed to do all in her power and succeeded. . After stubbornly resisting his son's wishes for two years, Matthew Vianney finally admitted defeat and gave his consent.

Now, Father Balley would have to be asked if he would accept one more student. And what a student! John Mary was now an ungainly youth of nineteen, with very little formal education.

Mary Vianney went with fear and trembling to see Father Balley, accompanied by her sister Margaret Humbert. The priest listened, seemed undecided what to say, and then answered:

"I am so busy, I just can't take on another student!"

As the women respectfully insisted, he said once more: "No, No! I just cannot do it."

The women decided to go and get reinforcements. Mary Vianney's son-in-law, Melin by name, lived in Ecully. He, too, came and pleaded with Father Balley on behalf of his brother-in-law.

As Father Balley was about to refuse him too, Melin said:

"At least, consent to see him. When you have seen him, I'm sure you'll accept him."

"Well then, let him come!"

And so John Mary Vianney came to Ecully. We are inclined to think there was something in his glance, in his face, in his whole demeanor, and especially in his smile, something so eloquent and compelling that one could not resist him. Father Balley saw him, questioned him, and then, as if thinking aloud, exclaimed:

"As for this one, I accept him!" Then he added, "Rest assured, my friend, I'm ready to make sacrifices for you if there is need."

And he kept his word.

A Faltering Memory

John Mary Vianney was not stupid. He understood things fast and well. Above all, he was endowed with great common sense and a keen power of observation. On the other hand, his memory was like a sieve. He just couldn't remember the fundamentals of Latin. The declensions and conjugations were impenetrable mysteries to him. He worked hard and prayed with all his might, but the results were almost nil. The small boys who were in his class couldn't understand why something that seemed like a game to them was so hard for him.

Matthias Loras, the brightest of Father Balley's pupils, once tried to help John Mary with his Latin. He became so impatient with his slowness that he slapped him violently in front of the others. What followed amazed everyone. The gawky twenty-year-old who also had a quick temper knelt down before the twelve-year-old comrade who had just slapped him, and humbly begged his forgiveness. This unexpected action on John Mary's part completely disarmed the younger boy. He threw his arms around him, and the two became lifelong friends.

Matthias Loras was to become a missionary in the United States, and eventually bishop of Dubuque, Iowa. His reputation for holiness was so great in his own diocese that there has been question of starting his beatification process. So it seems that Father Balley's rectory school was a place which produced saints.

One day, however, John Mary became discouraged. He thought God really didn't want him to be a priest since he couldn't learn anything. And so, with tear-filled eyes, he said to Father Balley:

"I want to go back home!"

That was all he could say in his state of dejection.

"Where do you want to go, my poor child?" his teacher asked gently. "You want to go and look for trouble.... You know that your father wants to keep you at home. When he sees how dejected you are he won't let you go away again. Then, it will be good-bye to all your hopes, John Mary! Good-bye to the priesthood and to the souls you wanted to help!"

Father Balley knew he was touching John Mary's weak point. The youth wept some more, but now it was because he was ashamed he had lost heart. He never said another word about leaving the school. At the same time, he felt the need of a more heroic form of prayer than he had so far used. He decided to make a pilgrimage to La Louvesc, begging his way, to implore the help of St. Francis Regis, the amazing seventeenth-century missionary of the Vivarais region of southeastern France.

This happened in 1806. It was a journey of some 100 kilometers (65 miles). John Mary set out on foot and at first tried to get along without eating or drinking. That soon proved to be beyond his strength. He was forced to beg for some bread. But this hearty twenty-year-old did not inspire compassion. Looking at him, the first thing people thought was that he should be working like everybody else. He was repulsed and insulted by everyone he approached for alms. So he continued his journey, eating herbs and quenching his thirst at springs and streams. He was about to drop from exhaustion when someone finally gave him a few crusts of bread. Strengthened with this food he was able to reach La Louvesc, situated at an altitude of 1,100 meters (about 3,600 feet) in the Haut-Vivarais mountains.

Once there, John Mary prayed with all his heart that St. Regis might obtain for him the grace to complete his studies. He had brought some money with him, and felt he should use it to return home, instead of begging his way back. His Jesuit confessor agreed to commute his begging vow on condition that he give alms instead of receiving them on the way home. This vow had proved so difficult to keep that in later years Father Vianney said: "I would never advise anyone to make a vow of begging." He added that he had learned from experience how truly Christ spoke when He said: "It is better to give than to receive."

The Deserter

At this point in our story we must recount a rather unusual episode in John Vianney's long and laborious preparation for the priesthood.

Cardinal Fesch, who was Napoleon's uncle and Archbishop of Lyons, had obtained exemption from

military service for all seminarians under his jurisdiction, including those who had not yet received
any of the priestly orders. Be this as it may, in the
fall of 1809 John Mary Vianney received his call to
the colors with an order to report at a military bar-
racks. This was a great surprise to him, as he had
been registered as a seminarian in 1807, the year
he was confirmed by Cardinal Fesch. Since then he
had been studying for the priesthood at the rectory
of Ecully. The reason he was not exempted from
military service as a seminarian was probably the
great need for troops to fight in Spain.

Father Balley's efforts to save John Mary from
military service were of no avail, nor did the certifi-
cate issued by the vicar general, Father Courbon,
regarding his ecclesiastical status, help. There was
nothing to do but answer the call to military service.
On October 26, 1809, Vianney arrived at the Lyons
military depot. Two days later he was taken sick with
a fever and transported to the hospital. For the next
two weeks he remained a patient at the hospital.
When members of his family came to visit him, he
kept talking to them of God and of his desire to do
His holy will.

On November 12th, a detachment was leaving
for Bayonne. John Mary was attached to the convoy
and put into uniform. But by the time they reached
Roanne he had to be placed in the hospital once more.
This time, he was hospitalized for six weeks. On
January 6, 1810, he was supposed to leave for the
Spanish frontier with other soldiers. But he could
not keep up with them. When he arrived at the
recruiting center he found the detachment had gone
off without him. The officer in charge, Captain Blanchard, was furious and spoke of putting him in chains.
But he quickly regained his composure and sent the
young recruit on his way with the command to join
his group in the company.

So our young draftee started hiking up the first ridges of the Madeleine Mountains. He was soon exhausted by the effort and by his recent illness, and lay down to rest in a wooded area. As he was reciting the rosary a young man came up to him.

"What are you doing here?" he asked. "Come with me."

In later years, Vianney told about it.

"He took my knapsack which was very heavy, and told me to follow him. We walked for a long time through the night, in between the trees of the mountain. I was so exhausted I could hardly keep up with him."

The young man was a deserter. He knew the countryside well, and like many other young men was hiding out to escape being drafted. They walked along together, chatting as they went.

"You certainly don't look much like a soldier," said the stranger.

"Yes, that's true. But I have to obey."

"If you want to follow me, you can hide out in our village which is entirely surrounded by forests."

"No, I couldn't do that. I've given my parents enough trouble already."

"Don't worry about it. Many others have hidden out in these parts."

And so our unwilling deserter was led to a small isolated house where he was given some food and the only bed in the place.

The next day John Mary went to the small town of Les Noës, to report his plight to the mayor. This magistrate, Paul Fayot, felt no obligation to apply the laws of the Empire. As it happened he was already hiding two deserters in his own home in the neighboring village of Les Robins. To accept a third would surely cause him embarrassment. Even so, he had pity on John Mary and decided to keep him in the village as the local schoolteacher. First, he gave him a new name. John Mary Vianney would now be known as Jerome Vincent. He was to stay at the home of the mayor's cousin, Claudine Fayot, a widow and a most charitable woman.

The first few months were the hardest. Despite his new identity, Jerome Vincent was always on the *qui vive.* He hid during the day, and went outside only in the evening when he would go to read the Gospel or the Lives of the Saints to the members of the family. He had soon won everyone by his charm and simplicity. He then began to teach reading, writing, catechism, to all who wanted to learn, whether young or old. He even dared go down to the town of Les Noës to attend the Mass that was said very early in the morning.

Our deserter lived in a state of great anxiety. What was happening in the plains? Wouldn't his parents be harassed with inquiries about his involuntary desertion? As he now saw it, his desertion was now permanent. There was no going back. After all, seminarians were exempt from military service, and he had been the victim of some oversight or error. Now Providence had found him a safe shelter. He felt he should allow himself to be guided by the local magistrate, namely, the mayor. An apostolate had been opened to him, since he had the chance to teach as well as to give the example of a prayerful and virtuous life. And so he stayed on. The gendarmes were never able to locate him. At times, it almost seemed as if he escaped their search through some sort of miracle.

In mid-summer, 1810, Mme. Fayot, his hostess, went to Charbonnières-les-Bains, near Lyons, to take a mineral water cure. One day, she appeared at the home of the Vianneys, bringing them a letter from their son. Madame Vianney was elated to hear from him, but Matthew made his annoyance very clear. The police were constantly harassing him and imposing fines on him because of his deserter-son.

"Where do you live" he asked Claudine Fayot, "so that I can go and get him?"

"Even if you knew where I live," she answered, "I would hide him somewhere else. He's worth more than everything you own."

In the end, John Mary stayed on at Les Robins. He was even able to send for his textbooks and resume his seminary studies. But he soon received some good news. The Emperor had just conquered Austria and, on the occasion of his marriage with the Austrian Archduchess Marie Louise, had granted amnesty to all deserters. The recruiting officer, Captain Blanchard, informed the Vianneys that their son would escape conscription if he could find a substitute. John Mary's younger brother Francis offered to take his place. As he had drawn a high number in the military lottery he had been deferred, but he agreed to enter the military service as a substitute for his brother in return for the promise of 3,000 francs out of their father's estate.

At last Jerome Vincent could resume his own identity and return to his family. This was probably early in January, 1811. His "time of sorrow and banishment" had lasted about a year. There were tearful farewells with the Fayots, because he had almost become like a beloved member of their family.

It should be noted, in closing this episode, that no one really thought John Mary Vianney had acted wrongly in becoming a deserter from the Army. And as for his own conscience which shunned the slightest sin or imperfection, it does not seem to have troubled him in any way. He did not think he had offended God by acting as he did.

Abbé Toccanier, who knew him intimately, has related that he never heard John Vianney condemn himself or try to justify his actions in the matter. "However, I heard him tell his own story during his catechism classes, by way of comparison. 'When I was a deserter I was always afraid the gendarmes would come and get me. Likewise, the sinner in his remorse always thinks he is about to be seized by divine justice.'"

But when Father Vianney said such things, there was not the slightest hint of contrition in his manner. Actually, under the Restoration which followed the Empire, to have been a deserter was considered an honor and something to boast about.

The Seminarian-
The Priest-
The Curate
at Ecully

Father Balley Again

No one was happier to see John Mary Vianney again than his teacher, Father Balley. This holy priest had never despaired of seeing him again. One day he had even told the youth's mother when she came for encouragement:

"Mother, don't worry about your son. He is neither dead nor sick. He will never be a soldier. He's going to be a priest."

Mme. Vianney believed his words, but she did not live to see the prophecy fulfilled. Soon after her son's return to Dardilly she died, but not before pleading successfully with her husband to let John Mary continue his priestly studies at Ecully.

This time Father Balley decided the young man was to tend the rectory garden during his spare time, and serve both as sacristan and altar boy. Meanwhile he would guide him more closely in his efforts to learn Latin.

Arrangements were made to have John Mary accepted as equal in rank to the students of rhetoric in the minor seminaries, and he received the tonsure on May 28, 1811. He was now a member of the clergy, and addressed as Abbé Vianney. Perhaps the most significant factor in his preparation for the priesthood was his close association with Father Balley — an admirable man of penance and prayer, as John Mary Vianney was also to be.

At the Seminary of Verrières

In those days students for the priesthood were required to have one year of philosophy and two years of theology. In October, 1812, John Mary Vianney was admitted to the *Petit Séminaire* of Verrières, near Montbrison, to study his philosophy. He was then over 26 years old, and by far the oldest student in his class. Even the professor was younger than he.

Father Balley's struggling protégé was soon among the least promising students at the seminary. The courses were given entirely in Latin, and he couldn't understand a word that was being said. Seven of the poorest learners were taken apart and taught the courses in French. John Mary was among them, but he still didn't understand much better than before.

Even so, about eight months later, in June, 1813, he felt confident enough to write to Father Balley: "My studies seem to be progressing a bit better than I had expected!"

John Mary remained in the lowest quartile of his class. He was truly one of those of whom St. Paul had said: "God has chosen the weak to confound the strong!"

He sought consolation in the seminary chapel, before the tabernacle. Prayer would always be his strong point, far more than the knowledge and wisdom of this world.

At the Major Seminary

The following summer, John Mary returned to Ecully, where he studied assiduously under his kind teacher, Father Balley. Then, in the autumn he entered the Major Seminary of *Saint-Irénée* in Lyons. He was taking another important step toward the priesthood.

Saint-Irénée stood high on Place Croix-Paquet, where now stands one of two funiculars going up Croix-Rousse Mountain. There is nothing left of the structure now, but it once was quite imposing. At that time it was surrounded by gardens and a beautiful avenue of lime trees. The Sulpicians had been driven out of the seminary by the decree of December 26, 1811, which dispossessed their society of all its seminaries in France. They had been replaced by diocesan priests, most of whom were quite young and brilliant. Two archbishops were to come from their ranks.

At *Saint-Irénée*, John Mary found one of his old school-friends from Verrières, Marcellinus Champagnat, the future founder of the Little Brothers of Mary. We should also mention two of his other colleagues: John Claude Colin, the future founder of the Society of Mary and a man of rare virtue, and Ferdinand Donnet, who would some day become Archbishop of Bordeaux and ultimately a Cardinal.

After a fervent retreat, the courses began shortly before All Saints' Day, 1813.

Several of the seminarians of that year would be called upon in later years to make despositions at the beatification process of Abbé Vianney. Not one of them could have foreseen such a possibility in 1813. And yet Vianney did not go unnoticed. He had two qualities that drew attention to him. On the one hand, his fervor, his spirit of recollection, his modesty, his total abnegation, his spirit of prayer and penance; and on the other hand, his great difficulty in keeping up with the courses. Thus, from one point of view, he had everything required to become a holy priest; and from another, his intellectual deficiencies were enough to keep him from ordination.

Father Declas, a Marist, later said of him: "I knew him very well in times past. He is certainly a saint!"

However, they all agreed that John Mary did everything he could to hide any outward appearance of holiness. There was "nothing extraordinary about his behavior. He was a very simple man."

He was not satisfied to pray long and hard. He also studied with all his might. He was always buried in his books. But his efforts brought few results. Needless to say, when he was spoken to in French, when his courses were "masticated" for him in a language he knew well, he understood, and when he was questioned he would give correct and meaningful answers.

Unfortunately, Latin was the official language of the seminary. John Mary had a hard time understanding what was said to him in Latin, and even greater difficulty trying to express himself in the language.

It was only with the help of a French-language manual called the *Rituel de Toulon*, that John Mary was able to acquire the basic knowledge indispensable for his future ministry.

Disaster Strikes

Although John Vianney was able to explain dogmas and solve moral problems when he was addressed in French, he was terrified at the thought of taking examinations. Whenever he had to appear before a panel of professors, he would become confused, frightened, paralyzed. His first examination at *Saint-Irénée* was a disaster. He had been at the Seminary several months. But as the teachers had

*Father John Vianney at thirty-two. Son of a farmer,
he was practical and down-to-earth. He was short but
robust, able to get by on five hours sleep a night.*

stopped questioning him in class, he was completely floored when he was interrogated during the examination. He received the lowest mark in the class, which was set down as D, the equivalent of zero. Anyone who received this mark was automatically excluded from further classes.

All John Mary's hopes were crumbling. He would never become a priest! He was dismissed from the seminary, and it seemed as though the decision was final.

Fifty years later, Cardinal Donnet was to say: "The memory of his humility and of the good sense he demonstrated in the conversation I had with him on that occasion has remained deeply etched in my mind."

Father Balley's Tenacity

Once again Father Balley saved the day. God had decreed that he was the man to give this great priest to His Church.

John Mary, in all humility, had accepted the terrible blow. Seeing himself unworthy of the priesthood, he immediately thought of entering another branch of God's service. Since he could not be a priest, he would become a religious Brother.

He remembered one of his comrades, John Dumond, who had received the habit of the Brothers of the Christian Schools on November 27, 1813. Even before he went to see Father Balley, he visited his old friend.

"I don't know enough Latin to become a priest," John Mary confided. "I'll come back here to become a Brother."

Then, convinced that he would be back in Lyons within a few days, he returned to Ecully.

With unabashed tears, he told Father Balley about his misfortune. The latter made no show of emotion. With incredible trust in God's plans, he resolved to go against the tide. He would seek permission to take his student back, so he could train him himself, and then submit him to the examinations of the seminary superiors. He realized how urgently priests were needed at that period of France's history. But above all, he sensed what sort of a priest this young man could become.

"Write to your friend in Lyons," Father Balley advised John Mary. "Tell him I want you to continue your studies."

John Mary obeyed. The Christian Brothers were informed of his new plans. Father Balley began to teach him again with the *Rituel de Toulon*. Now, more than ever, prayer alternated with study in his life, or rather, the two were fused as one.

Heaven's Answer

Such courage, fidelity, and faith finally brought a response from God's Providence.

Later on, our saint recounted: "I was overwhelmed with a great sadness. I didn't know what to do about it.... I can still see the exact spot in Ecully—I was passing by the house of the widow Bibost. I heard words spoken to me as clearly as if they had been uttered in my ear: 'Come now, don't worry! You will be a priest some day!'"

Strengthened by this reassurance, John Mary redoubled his efforts. Three months later, another examination was given at the Seminary *Saint-Irénée*. Father Balley arranged for his protégé to take it. Alas! When John Mary's turn came to be questioned, he acted exactly as he had on the previous occasions. He panicked, stammered, and gave vague, unsatisfactory answers to the questions put to him.

As the panel of professors held Father Balley in high respect, it was decided that though John Mary Vianney could not be accepted by the Archdiocese of Lyons, he would be free to ask for admission in some other diocese.

Father Balley did not accept defeat. He asked the panel to come to Ecully and interrogate his candidate there, in his presence. In view of his reputation in the Archdiocese, he was granted this exceptional favor.

When the panel came to Ecully, Father Bochard and Father Gardette, the superior of the major seminary, were amazed at the miracle they witnessed.

In a supportive atmosphere that built up his self-confidence John Mary could summon all of his limited intellectual resources for the great test. It was· recorded that "he answered the questions put to him very well, and the panel was satisfied with his answers."

Father Courbon was then the administrator of the Archdiocese, acting in the name of Cardinal Fesch who had been exiled when his nephew Napoleon abdicated. It was Father Courbon who had to decide on John Mary's future. When he received the report given him by Father Bochard, he weighed the Archdiocese's dire need for priests against the seminarian's obvious deficiencies.

Finally, he looked at Father Bochard and asked: "Is Abbé Vianney a devout man? Does he have devotion to the Blessed Virgin Mary? Can he recite his rosary?"

"Why yes, he is a model of piety!"

"A model of piety! Well then, I accept him. The grace of God will do the rest!"

Father Balley had won his battle, and the Church of France had won a saint.

The Subdiaconate

As we have already noted, John Mary Vianney had received the tonsure in 1811. This is not one of the Orders, but the preamble to Orders. He was to receive the minor Orders, and by a special dispensation be admitted to the subdiaconate the same day and during the same ceremony. The ordination took place on July 2, 1814. The ordaining prelate was Bishop Simon, the first bishop of Grenoble under the Concordat, who had come expressly from Lyons for the occasion.

The subdiaconate was what we might call the decisive step, for it is the first of the major Orders. At that time, it involved taking the vow of celibacy, the obligation to recite the breviary, and was a definitive commitment to the priesthood. In entering this state, a young man gave himself totally to God.

Obviously, history can only record externals, such as dates and places. It cannot reveal what goes on in men's hearts. What happened to John Mary Vianney on that day when, after so many trials, doubts, uncertainties and anxieties, he experienced the joy of consecrating himself totally to Jesus Christ? What hymns of adoration, blessing, and petition did his soul sing to his gentle Master? We do not know, and yet that would be the real story of that day.

However, we have the testimony of Abbé Pierre Millon, pastor of Bény, given in later years.

"I had the good fortune to be very close to Abbé Vianney that day. After the ceremony, it was customary to go in procession from the cathedral to the seminary. I was struck by the enthusiasm with which he sang the *Benedictus*, the Psalm of thanksgiving. His face was radiant. Inwardly, I applied to him the verse: 'And you, child, shall be a prophet of the Most High!' thinking to myself: he has less knowledge than some others, but he will do great things in the sacred ministry."

Father Balley Keeps Trying

The Archdiocesan authorities were impressed by the success of Father Balley's student. They wisely decided to entrust to him the final preparation of his protégé for the priesthood. John Mary was not to return to the seminary until his retreats before ordination to the diaconate, and then to the priesthood. He spent the scholastic year 1814-1815 at Ecully, and was thus sheltered from the excitement that political events were arousing at the Seminary *Saint-Irénée*.

The year 1814-1815 was the time of the first Restoration. First, there were the delirious enthusiasms of the monarchists soon followed by Napoleon's return from the Island of Elba, including his triumphal march from the Jouan Gulf to Paris, by way of Lyons. Then came the Belgian campaign, and finally Waterloo, the fall of the Emperor, his departure for Saint Helena, and the second Restoration which at first meant foreign occupation.

Cardinal Fesch, who had been driven from France, returned to Lyons, but only for three days. He had to go into exile again after his nephew's second abdication. He was to die in Rome on May 13, 1839, still clinging to his title as Archbishop of Lyons.

The seminarians had followed these events with youthful enthusiasm. As a result, scholastically speaking the year left much to be desired. John Mary Vianney was truly fortunate to be away from these disturbing national trends.

Toward the end of May, 1815, during the Hundred Days, Vianney returned to the seminary to prepare for the diaconate. He received this Order, which confers the Holy Spirit and the spirit of strength, on June 23rd, five days after the Battle of Waterloo. Bishop Simon ordained him in the cathedral of St. John.

The Priesthood

The great day was fast approaching. Soon John Mary Vianney would be a priest. We have no records of what was going on within him at this time. We can only conjecture that his heart was filled with holy aspirations, and overflowing with acts of humility and love.

We can assume, with little chance of being wrong, that his daily recitation of the breviary since the time of his ordination to the subdiaconate had obtained immense graces from heaven for him. The biographers make no mention of this. But the evidence is clear. This poor young man who knew so little Latin, yet had such great fervor and supernatural insights, recited his divine office with utmost devotion. He was not satisfied to read all those Latin Psalms, antiphons, stories of the saints and patristic homilies. He was determined to understand what he read, savor it, nourish his heart and mind with it. Those who saw him recite his breviary, later testified to this. He said it on his knees, and with unwavering attention. His face betrayed his emotion and fervor. Sometimes he would pause, as if suspended before a word or verse of the Psalms that was more profound or sublime than the rest.

Under the guidance of Father Balley, it is certain that he learned much of the "science of the saints" by reciting his breviary. It seemed that even Latin, which had been so hard for him, had now become quite familiar.

We need not be surprised, therefore, that when Father Bochard returned to Ecully to give John Mary his final examination for the priesthood, he found the young man had made amazing progress since the preceding year. He questioned Vianney in great detail for over an hour on the most delicate points of morals. The answers were uniformly clear and correct. And so John Mary Vianney was accepted for the priesthood. He went alone to Grenoble to be ordained, because his fellow-students Marcellinus Champagnat and John Claude Colin still had another year of preparation.

However, as a precaution, Vianney was ordained with the faculties to say Mass, but not to hear confessions. Who would have foreseen at that moment that he was to spend the better part of his life in the confessional!

John Mary set out on foot and alone, and covered the 100 kilometers (64 miles) under the hot August sun. He had to travel through an area infested with Austrian soldiers who often shouted insults at him as he passed, insults he did not understand but quietly offered up to his God.

On Saturday evening, August 12, 1815, he was welcomed at the major seminary of Grenoble. The ordination took place the following day. When Bishop Simon was told that there was only this deacon from Lyons to ordain, he answered:

"It is certainly never too much trouble to ordain a good priest!"

He did not know how truly he spoke.

Once again, we do not know the essentials of that occasion. We have no record of what God said to His new priest, and what the young priest said to his God. From early childhood, John Mary had carried on an almost continuous dialogue with God, except when he was sleeping. He had really been in a state of "perpetual" prayer, as the traditional prayer for his feast expresses it. But there were certainly higher and more luminous peaks of union with God, especially at turning points in his life. Of these, we unfortunately know nothing.

The best we can do is to join Abbé Francis Trochu, his principal biographer, in citing what John Mary Vianney said himself about the priesthood:

"Oh! How great a person is the priest! The priest will truly understand himself only when he gets to heaven.... If we understood what the priesthood means, we would die, not from fright, but from love!"

The day was August 13, 1815, the thirteenth Sunday after Pentecost. John Mary Vianney was now a priest forever. And he was among those who would do honor to their priesthood. Rarely has it been more truly said of a priest: *Sacerdos alter Christus!* The priest is another Jesus Christ!

His First Masses

The ordination ceremony had taken place in the chapel of the Major Seminary of Grenoble. It was there that Abbé Vianney said his first Mass, and we can imagine his fervor on that occasion. He chose to say the Mass of August 15th, for the feast of the Assumption of the Blessed Virgin in the same chapel. Most probably, he did not return to Ecully until several days later. It was a two or three day's walk from Grenoble to Lyons, and he was subjected to the same affronts from the Austrian soldiers as before.

When he arrived at Father Balley's rectory, he was delighted to learn that he had been appointed to be the curate at Ecully.

So John Mary would not have to leave the man who was his great friend, and to whom, after God, he owed his priestly vocation, the man who had never given up on him even in the darkest days. Now, he was to be this man's associate, his co-worker. There would still be opportunity to learn from his teaching and his example. This must be seen as another of God's providential acts on his behalf.

Father Vianney said his first solemn Mass at Ecully. His friends from Les Robins and Les Noës had been invited. At Dardilly, the entire Vianney family was filled with excitement. This family knew what a great honor it was to have a priest in the family. It is hard for us to realize how intensely the flame of faith burned in the Christian families which had passed through the crucible of the French Revolution and its aftermath.

Pastor and Curate

It would be even harder for us to envisage the spirit of faith that reigned in France's humble rectories in those days. Father Balley had never emigrated. During the terror he had risked his life a hundred times. Disguised as a carpenter, he had continued his sacred ministry. Not only did he prove his courage outwardly. His was a profound inner faith, and he knew how to communicate it to his disciple, his beloved son, now his curate.

At that time there was perhaps not much talk of the "Mystical Body" of the Church. But many of the elements of this doctrine were already understood and practiced. For instance, the dogma of the "communion of saints," of the reversibility of merits, of the reparation faithful Christians need to make for those who revolt and become apostates. Likewise, the doctrine of the moral unity that exists in the Church between the just and sinners, between the "good" and the "wicked." All these teachings were understood, preached, and practiced with great intensity by the Curé of Ars. If we reread the writings of Joseph de Maistre, we will see that these doctrines were very popular at that time.

Abbé Vianney spent two and a half years as curate of Ecully, in close community with his kind teacher and pastor. Together they practiced rigorous penance, prayed, and spent long hours talking about spiritual and doctrinal matters. Father Balley was an ascetic man. We might even be tempted to say he was a "formidable" ascetic, inasmuch as he lived a life of such strict fasting and penance as to frighten less hardy souls. He wore a hairshirt, flogged himself, and practiced continual mortification at mealtime.

In the rectory at Ecully, the favorite reading consisted of the Holy Bible, the *Lives of the Saints*, and above all, the *Lives* of the early Desert Fathers. Here the two priests culled examples of the victory of spirit over the flesh, victories that terrify us today. When we delve into the writings of John Cassian, for example, we are inclined to agree with the Gaulish monks referred to by Sulpicius-Severus, who was St. Martin's biographer:

"But we are Gauls, and we have hearty appetites! We cannot imitate what these Egyptian monks have done, for they were never hungry!"

Father Balley and his disciple were true "Gauls," but they fought their hunger and thirst and the need for sleep, as well as their love of comfort and the desires of the flesh. Of course, they did not depend on their own strength in these struggles, but placed their trust first and above all in God's grace. That is what we discern when we read the memoirs of Abbé Talhades of Montpellier, written in 1839. In them we read:

"On October 3, 1838, Abbé Vianney made a very important revelation to me. I asked how he had succeeded in overcoming temptations against chastity. He finally avowed that it was the result of a vow. He had made the vow twenty-three years earlier, in 1816, when he was a curate at Ecully. It consisted in the daily recitation of the *Regina coeli* (Rejoice, O Queen of Heaven....) and reciting six times daily the prayer: 'Blessed be forever the most holy and immaculate Conception of the Blessed Virgin Mary, Mother of God! Amen.'"

In any event, a reading of the life of the Curé of Ars will quickly dispel any notion that there is any easy way to become a saint. Easy solutions are of no use either in the things of this world or in those of the spirit. But in the life of John Mary Vianney, we have an added proof of the major role Father Balley played in leading him to holiness.

We have the Curé of Ars' own word for it:

"I would finally have acquired a little wisdom if I had had the good fortune to remain with Father Balley always. No one made me see so clearly to what degree the soul can free itself of the senses, and man can approach the angelic life.... Just to hear him say: 'My God, I love you with all my heart,' was enough to make anyone love God too."

After Father Balley's example, the young curate also decided to wear a hairshirt. Like his pastor, he often flogged himself. Like him, too, he placed his trust in mortification, penance, acts of reparation and expiation, in order to convert sinners. Like him, he reduced the needs of the body to a minimum at meal-time. When they sat down to eat, there was, as it were, a battle of generosity between the two as to who would make the greatest penance. They drank no wine, and were satisfied to eat potatoes and dark bread. When some boiled meat was served, neither of them touched it. Afterwards, it would be given to the needy.

They went to such extremes that their parishioners reported both the pastor and his curate to the Archbishop's office, accusing them of practicing such excessive mortification as to ruin their health. Things went even further. The pastor secretly reported his curate, and the curate reported his pastor, on the same count.

Father Courbon of the Archbishop's office found the whole matter quite amusing. His answer to the parishioners confirms what we said earlier about the popularity of the doctrine of the Mystical Body at that time:

"People of Ecully, you are indeed fortunate to have priests doing so much penance for you!"

This is something for us to remember. The penance practiced by pastors was considered a source of blessings for their parishioners!

The Power of the Keys

The rectory at Ecully was not only a school of holiness for Abbé Vianney. It was also a kind of annex to the seminary. It was there that he had learned the few fundamentals that his faulty memory was able to store away. It was there that he reviewed, complemented, and completed his pastoral studies. In a word, Ecully was in a sense the novitiate of the Curé of Ars.

At his ordination to the priesthood, he had not been granted the faculty of hearing confessions. But this prohibition did not last very long. All that was probably needed, was a quick review of the *Rituel di Toulon*, and a chance for the pastor to make sure his curate knew the fundamentals needed for the tribunal of penance. Very soon, he was asking his curate to hear his confessions, as though to test his capacities. And once satisfied as to the young priest's adequacy, he requested the full powers of the keys for the man so many souls had been waiting for.

As soon as Abbé Vianney had the faculty to hear confessions, penitents began to throng to his confessional. And after they had been to him once, they kept coming back to their great spiritual benefit.

Father Balley was in no sense jealous of his young colleague. He kept ceding more and more of his activities to his associate. He was happy and proud to have trained such a competent successor. The time had come when he could sing his *Nunc dimittis* "Now, Master, you can dismiss your servant in peace" (Lk. 2:29-32).

The Death of Father Balley

The good and faithful teacher had earned his reward. The hardships he had endured during the French Revolution, the long vigils at a time when he was forced to practice his ministry under cover of night, his uncounted mortifications and penances all contributed to shorten his life. By February, 1817, when he was only 65 years old, he was almost completely immobilized by an ulcerated leg, evidently the result of very poor circulation—this, in turn, the result of his many privations. During the entire year, 1817, we have the record of only one parochial document bearing his signature. All the others were signed by his curate.

The ulcer became infected, and gangrene set in. The local physicians gave up hope of curing him.

In December, 1817, the curate administered the last rites to his pastor. For this solemn action, he convoked the most faithful parishioners, as was then customary. The farewells must have been filled with great emotion. It was the leave-taking of a saint.

After the parishioners had gone home, the scene became more poignant. The dying man gave his "dear son" his parting counsels, and asked for his prayers. Then, pulling out his instruments of penance from under his pillow, he said:

"Take these things, my poor child, and hide them. If these objects were found after my death, people would think I had sufficiently expiated my sins. And then they'd leave me in purgatory until the end of the world."

With these words, he handed his discipline and his hairshirt to John Mary, a precious legacy from a great father to a great son.

Speaking of Father Balley, the Curé of Ars said later: "I have encountered beautiful souls, but never any more beautiful than his."

Among the greatest favors God had granted John Mary Vianney was the opportunity to meet and know Father Balley on the road of life.

It seems that a few of the parishioners expressed the wish to have Father Vianney as their pastor. He, for one, did not want it, because he considered the parish far too important for him. Father Balley's successor was Father Tripier, who was still a young man. He had no need of a curate, and so the one he had was soon sent away. In February, 1818, less

than two months after the death of Father Balley
(which occurred on December 17, 1817), Abbé
Vianney was summoned to the Archbishop's house
to be told he had been appointed as chaplain-pastor
of Ars, in the Dombes region.

As Father Courbon signed the appointment,
he said simply: "There isn't much love of God
in that parish. You will put some love of God into it!"

The Conquest of Ars

A Poor Parish

Although Ars was a township, it could scarcely be called a parish. Its village church was really only a mission chapel attached to the nearby parish of Misérieux, three kilometers (about two miles) away. However, its chaplain was called a pastor. The commune paid him the very modest salary of 500 francs a year. The surplus fees probably never exceeded 50 francs a year. Fortunately Ars had its château where dwelt a very charitable and devout lady, Mademoiselle des Garets d'Ars, whose help to the parish was to prove providential.

Ars was truly one of the poorest parishes of France, in terms of material resources. It was equally poor from the spiritual point of view.

Here is a picture of Father Vianney's first parish. The church was small and somewhat dilapidated. There was almost no religious fervor among the people. They were not hostile, but simply indifferent, and this was perhaps worse than genuine hostility. The youth of the place had a great love of dancing. Dances were held quite often, on Sundays and holidays, and they were so widely known that people came to them from neighboring villages. In this hamlet of less than 200 souls there were four taverns, where drunken revelry held sway.

To put it candidly, Ars had known better days from the point of view of religion. Here the traditions of "Old France" had once thrived. There had been patriarchal families in which prayer in common was a regular practice, and which brought up their children to fear the Lord and honor the Christian virtues. But the Revolution had swept through the region, leaving an aftermath of spiritual and material destruction. The pastor who had preceded Abbé Vianney had lived there only twenty-three days, for he was dying of tuberculosis when he arrived. Except for Mlle. d'Ars, practically no one cared whether or not he would be replaced by another priest.

On the Way to Ars

On the morning of February 9, 1818, Abbé John Mary Vianney was traveling toward his humble parish. His few possessions had been hoisted into a cart, and included a bed frame, a clothes chest, and the books inherited from Father Balley. The new pastor followed along on foot, in the company of "Mère Bibost," an excellent woman from Ecully who had offered to help settle him in his new home, but was to remain only briefly at Ars.

What did the new Curé of Ars look like?

He was in his thirty-second year. He was very thin, and his furrowed, emaciated, sunken face showed the marks of continual privations. He was a little below medium height for a Frenchman of his time—1 m. 58 (5 ft. 2 in.). His forehead was broad and high. He had a heavy head of curly auburn hair which fell in waves to his shoulders. It would not take many years for his hair to turn prematurely white.

His bright blue eyes were his most striking feature. They reflected a remarkably gentle and yet vivacious personality. Everyone who looked into those eyes felt a mysterious emotion. It was as if his gaze penetrated deep into other men's hearts and consciences.

He was sturdily built, and walked with a rapid gait. He was quick and vigorous. He was also a bit nervous, and a barely noticeable tic made his left hand tremble.

Let us spend this day of February 9th with him, which was to be the most important turning point in his life. The unpretentious procession set out from Ecully toward the bridge over the Saône River at Lyons-Vaise. Then it followed the left bank of the river, passing through Fontaines, Rochetaillée, and Neuville-sur-Saône. Then, turning away from the river bank, the little group passed through Parcieux, Reyrieux, and Toussieux. Following the dirt roads, our travelers came to within a few miles of Ars, although they did not realize it. They had been walking five or six hours and were now tired. They looked around for someone to show them the way to Ars, but saw no one. They were lost. Father Vianney scanned the horizon and caught a glimpse of some children tending their animals. He went over to them, asked them for directions, but couldn't seem to make them understand. Finally one of the boys, Anthony Givre, showed him the way to Ars.

"My little friend," Abbé Vianney said to him, "you have shown me the road to Ars; *I will show you the road to heaven!*"

The very first words he spoke in his new parish revealed his purpose in coming there and how he understood his responsibilities as a pastor.

As the young shepherd had told him he was just on the edge of his new parish, Abbé Vianney knelt on the ground and uttered a fervent prayer. He had now taken possession of the battlefield.

stitution de
se d' ARS
rivée du st Curé

*The parish church of Ars as it looked when Fr. Vianney
arrived to begin his ministry. This church had to be
greatly enlarged during his lifetime.*

They continued their journey down to the banks of the Fontblin River. In the wintry mist, they could see the thatched roofs of a few cottages clustered around a simple chapel. That was Ars.

The next morning, February 10, the chapel bells rang out to announce Mass. The people of the village had learned of the new pastor's arrival the night before. The more remote homes were apprized of the news by the chiming of the bells.

The formal installation of the new pastor took place the following Sunday, February 13th. The pastor of the neighboring town of Misérieux, Father Ducreux, presided. The whole parish was present, and everyone kept their eyes on the newcomer. Even in that first sermon he told them how much he loved them, how much he yearned to bring them spiritual enrichment.

The first impression was favorable. Monsieur Mandy, the mayor of the village, reacted immediately, saying:

"We have only a poor church, but we have a holy pastor." In the following years he was to be one of Father Vianney's firmest supporters in the work of reform and renewal that Ars needed so much.

The "holy pastor" had little concern about his new lodgings. He left it up to *Mère Bibost* to set everything in place, and it was quickly done. Naturally, there was already some furniture in the rectory, awaiting the pastor. There was even an air of luxury about the place, because the neighboring château had lent a few rather beautiful pieces to enhance it. One of the first things the new pastor did was to return to the château whatever shocked his love of simplicity and poverty. He consented to keep only the strictly necessary.

Visitors to Ars nowadays can still form a good idea of the meager furnishings among which Abbé

Vianney lived. Every effort has wisely been made to preserve everything as it was when he lived there, or to restore things to their original state at the time of his death.

During those first days, the parishioners were probably impressed by the selflessness, detachment, and renouncement they witnessed in the young priest. But they had no inkling of the great impact their young pastor would have on their lives.

The Weapons of the Curé of Ars

Let us think for a moment about an amazing series of facts: a thirty-two-year-old pastor arrived in a village with a population of 200, until then unknown to the world. He transformed this village from top to bottom so completely that people could say: *Ars is no longer Ars.* Then he went on to make of this unattractive and unknown village the focus of a world-wide pilgrimage.

When we think of these things, can we fail to see that some sort of a miracle of the moral order occurred here? Who could have foreseen such a transfiguration, such a resurrection and ascension? Father Vianney would have been the last, in his humility, to dream of any such brilliant success for his ministry. A time would come when he understood that God in His mercy was making use of him to work miracles. He was much too realistic and clearheaded not to realize this, but it only deepened his humility. He simply felt that God chooses the most wretched in preference to the more talented. His habitual attitude was always true to the French School of spirituality: to stand before God, engulfed ir his own nothingness.

In later years when he sought to explain to the crowds the wonders and miracles that drew pilgrims to Ars from everywhere, he attributed them to his devotion to little St. Philomena (the name means:

nameless), a young unknown martyr of the early Church, whom he had learned about in Ecully from Pauline Jaricot.[1]

And yet, as we tell the story of Abbé Vianney's life, we must not confuse our dates. The glories of Ars and of its pastor were to come much later, in their time. Before the glories there were ten years of frightful struggles, battles fought on a very small terrain it is true, but that were truly gigantic in their import.

Abbé Vianney was a giant of prayer and penance. His life gave external consistency, one might say, to the conditions that apply in every parish apostolate. A life-and-death duel was fought between him, the representative of Jesus Christ, and Satan who held sway over so many souls in that parish. And Satan could not resist making himself known in person, and making himself heard. The devil actually attacked this frail pastor who had dared confront him and was making him retreat all along the line of battle.

When we look at the life of the Curé of Ars from this angle of vision, it is a kind of revelation. That is why we need to take a very close look at it.

Prayer

We have already referred several times to John Mary Vianney's love of prayer. As time went on, prayer became the most important force in his life. His entire past life, all of his training and education, everything he had learned from Father Balley, can be summed up in a few words: I am nothing, God is everything. I can do nothing of myself, God can do everything. The souls of men belong to God, they were made for God. And the reason I came into the world, the reason I am here is to give them to God!

1. Mlle. Jaricot is known for having founded the Association for the Propagation of the Faith in Lyons, France in the year 1809.

Like all great mystics, Father Vianney possessed the virtue of humility to a heroic degree. The closer he came to God, the more he realized his wretchedness. It would seem he was never seriously tempted to pride. Quite the contrary. On many occasions he had to battle despair, the depressing sense of his nothingness, his unworthiness, his overwhelming need of going to some solitary place "to weep over his poor sins," to purify his "poor life."

However, he never succumbed to the horrible temptation to flee his responsibilities. Each time he was about to run away, he was held back or brought back by obedience, which is another way of saying, by humility.

Humility was the first mark of his prayer. Trust was the second. The third was constancy or fidelity. Perhaps it would be better to use the word chosen by the Church to describe it: *perpetuity.* John Mary Vianney's life was a continual prayer. He lived with God, in God. There was never any eclipse to his union with God. Everything we say about him in what follows should be understood in this light. He literally "lost" himself in God. His life exemplified Christ's sublime words: "Whoever loses his life for my sake will find it" (Mt. 16:25).

Where the Curé of Ars Prayed

We have no way of knowing what went on in John Vianney's heart-to-heart dialogue with God. Once again we are obliged to conjecture from the outward signs observed by others.

He was caught "in the act" of prayer practically everywhere. First of all in his church. Long before daybreak he would rise from his hard, narrow bed after a few hours sleep. Then, lantern in hand, he would go over to the church by way of the cemetery that surrounded it. After entering the church he would go straight to the tabernacle and prostrate himself on the floor. In that position he would pray. To use the words Blessed Jordan of Saxony applied to his master St. Dominic, he would "roar before the Lord." We can surmise his prayer went something like this:

"Dear God, I beg you to grant the conversion of my parish! I am willing to suffer anything you want and as long as I live! Yes, I'm willing to suffer for a hundred years the most excruciating pain, if only they are converted!"

He also shed many tears in the presence of his Jesus. When the sun rose, he was always there. Passers-by could see the flickering light of his lantern through the church windows. After his Mass, which he celebrated with the faith and love of an archangel, he would remain there in the church all morning. When he couldn't be found in the rectory, everybody knew where he was. He was praying before the tabernacle. There were even times when he spent the whole day there, forgetting about meals, and returned to the house only after the evening *Angelus.*

As a rule, however, he devoted several hours each day to visiting his parishioners. He used to go to see them at their homes, especially at mealtime, to be sure he would find the whole family together. He rarely ate anything himself. Turning to each member of the family, he would think of something pleasant and witty to say.

In his goings and comings he often traveled along isolated roads or in the woods. He would take advantage of the quiet and solitude to lose himself in intense prayer. He recited his breviary, the prayer of the universal Church, to which he was particularly devoted. And he would address this official prayer above all to the most holy and august Trinity. In fact, he always had a picture symbolizing the Trinity on the first page of his breviary. Catherine

Lassagne, the person who knew him best, has said: "The first virtue of *Monsieur le Curé* was *his faith in the Holy Trinity!*"

Devotion to God-Trinity was the foundation of his profound, robust, solid, and deeply theological piety, in the spirit of the purest Catholic tradition. We shall say more about it when we discuss his "spirituality."

After finishing his breviary, he recited the rosary. This was one of his favorite spiritual weapons. As we saw earlier, the Blessed Virgin Mary had been his first love. But during all his prayers, and amid his heartfelt cries to the heart of Jesus, he never for a minute forgot the parish he had been sent to convert. One day, as Monsieur Mandy, the mayor of Ars, was crossing a woods, he caught sight of the Curé through the trees, and saw he was on his knees. The mayor hid himself from view so as not to disturb him, but watched and listened. The young priest was weeping, and, unaware that he was being observed, kept repeating aloud: "O my God, convert my parish!"

The worthy peasant was touched to the core of his being, and slipped away quietly. But he promised himself to help his holy pastor with all his might to restore the village's spiritual vigor.

Penance

The Gospel records certain of Christ's words which the Curé of Ars must have studied with special attention, probably under the guidance of Father Balley, his spiritual master. These are the words Jesus spoke to the apostles concerning a demon they had been unable to exorcise: "This kind does not leave but by *prayer* and *fasting*" (Mt. 17:21).

We know the great importance Abbé Vianney attributed to these words from an answer he gave to one of his fellow pastors who had expressed his disappointment at not being able to convert his own parish.

"Have you prayed? Have you fasted?" he asked.

The best proof of all can be found in his actions. We have already said he was "a giant of prayer." He was also "a giant of penance."

As soon as *Mère Bibost* had returned to Ecully, which was probably two weeks after they arrived in Ars, he began doing penance to his heart's content. In his rectory, separated from the houses of the village, he was alone in the presence of his God, with no witnesses. He was free to engage in the most terrifying austerities.

He decided to sleep in a corner of his kitchen. In lieu of a bed, he spread out a few faggots on which he rested when he was starved for sleep. It was a very damp place, causing him to develop facial neuralgia which was one of his more serious crosses for over fifteen years. When unbearable pain drove him out of this corner of the first floor, he took refuge in the attic where he would lie down on the bare floor, and rest his aching head against a wooden log.

But before allowing himself this scant rest, he almost always began by flogging himself without mercy. He improvised his own instruments of penance, and was obliged to repair them frequently because he used them so violently. Blood would often spurt from his naked shoulders.

Catherine Lassagne has written about it: "It was pitiful to see the left shoulder of his shirts all hacked up and stained with blood." He must have fainted more than once during his scourgings, as witnessed by the bloody stains on the walls in a corner of his room, hidden behind a curtain.

But in accordance with the words of the Gospel, his principal penance consisted in fasting. Much has been said about the boiled potatoes he would cook early in the week and keep on eating until they were mildewed. This actually happened early in his ministry at Ars. In later years he would refer to it as one of the "follies" of his youth. "When one is young," he avowed, "one does many imprudent things."

In 1839, when Father Tailhades of Montpellier came to consult him on the secret of his pastoral conquests, he gave this candid answer:

"My friend, the Devil cares very little about discipline and other instruments of penance. What really puts him to rout is sacrificing one's need to drink, eat, and sleep. These are the penances the Devil dreads most and that are therefore most pleasing to God. Oh! How I experienced it! When I was alone, as I was indeed for eight or nine years, I was free to follow my bent. In fact, there were times when I didn't eat for whole days at a time.... Then God would grant me everything I wanted for myself as well as for others...."

As he spoke, he wept. Then he added:

"Now it is not quite the same any more. I am unable to remain without food as long as I used to, it reduces me to a state in which I can't talk any more.... But I was truly happy when I was alone! I would buy from beggars for my own use the bread that had been given them; I would spend the greater part of the night in the church; I didn't have as many confessions to hear then as I do now...and the good God used to grant me extraordinary graces...."

There is a wealth of insight in this admission. First, it shows us what Abbé Vianney thought of his life. In his eyes it was a hand-to-hand combat with the Devil. In conquering the Devil, he discovered that the discipline was less powerful than prayer and fasting. This is in perfect accord with the Gospels.

The Gospels make no mention of self-scourging with a "discipline," for example. Even St. Paul's *castigo corpus meum* ("What I do is discipline my own body and master it" [1 Cor. 9:27]) can be interpreted as fasting rather than using the "discipline." On the other hand, the Gospel speaks constantly of prayer and often of fasting. Christ's battle against Satan in the desert unfolded in a context of prayer and fasting.

In the second place, when the Curé of Ars had reached the glorious period of his earthly pilgrimage he missed the happiness of his early years of solitude. "How happy I was when I was alone!" he would say. This is surely a heartfelt cry. The crowds did not turn his head with illusions of fame.

Thirdly, he had the good sense to abandon or cut down his austerities when he saw they could be harmful to his ministry by depriving him of the strength he needed to carry on. He continued to demand the maximum of himself, but he was forced to admit: "I cannot stay so long without eating; it reduces me to a state in which I can't talk any more!" So he saw in this a sign of God's will for him.

There was another aspect of his penance related to his understanding of the doctrine of the Mystical Body of Christ. It deserves our attention now.

The Mystical Body

As we have already pointed out, there was already a widespread interest in the Mystical Body as a matter of practice, although its theological foundations were less discussed than they are today. When Abbé Vianney arrived at his parish he knew that he was united as one with his parishioners, that he would answer for them before God, that his functions as pastor involved doing penance for the salvation of their souls, offering reparation and satisfaction for their sins, their vices.

When he looked around him and saw his new parish in a state of decadence, he thought he would never be able to do enough penance to "redeem," like another Christ, these baptized Catholic Christians who had become for all practical purposes apostates, renegades to their faith.

He felt that he was not only God's representative before men, but also the representative of a sinful parish before God. Although he never spoke about the Mystical Body as such, he had a deep understanding of what it meant. And he acted accordingly. As time went on, however, he reduced the stringency of his penitential practices because of two considerations. First of all, once the parish had been conquered for Christ, there was less need of such penance; secondly, he had learned that excessive penance threatened his capacity to carry out his pastoral duties.

With regard to food, he gave up his earliest austerities. Of course, he was never to be a gourmet or a heavy eater. In time, he did allow the cook at *La Providence*, the school for girls he had founded, to prepare his meals. His famous pot for boiling potatoes was put away for good.

With the same practical common sense he allowed the sacristy to be heated and a fire to be lit in his bedroom, at least during the coldest weather.

Looking back at the "follies of his youth," as he called them, he did not repent of them as excessive, but missed them as a source of joy no longer open to him. Gradually they had given way to a more moderate outlook. Actually, his penances had not diminished. They had just taken on other forms, no less awesome to us when we think about them.

How His Preaching Developed

We find a similar evolution in his preaching. Among his pastoral duties, Father Vianney considered preaching from the pulpit one of the most important.

He had begun preaching at Ecully. And from what we can learn about it, it seems his sermons there were simple, clear, and brief. His sister Margaret, whom we have referred to earlier as little Gothon, admitted he was not an eloquent speaker. But, she added, in spite of this fact people thronged the church when they knew he was going to preach.

In the pulpit Father Vianney spoke in a rather high nasal tone that carried well. After he came to Ars, he continued to preach clearly and simply, often using colorful images to make his point, but his sermons became quite long.

His ministry was so successful that an effort was made to collect his sermons, at least those of the earlier years. They now make up five bound volumes. However we must admit that we can find little in them of unusual interest. Obviously they give us samples of his manner, his personal recollections, and insights into his character, which reveal the mind and heart of a saint. The fact remains that they really are of no great value to us from the point of view of doctrinal content or as models of how the great Christian truths should be presented.

The real worth of the Curé of Ars' sermons rested less in their content than in the tone and accents in which he preached them. His oratorical mimicry, his gestures, the intensity of his conviction, the very sight of the little pastor in the pulpit were more effective and efficacious than what he actually said. A time would come when his voice was so weakened with age that even those closest to the pulpit had difficulty understanding his sermons. Even so, there were tears in everyone's eyes as soon as he began to speak. Souls were touched, transpierced, and conversions were worked by the power of his holiness much more than by the appeal of his arguments.

It has been said that the best preacher is the one who loves God most. These words certainly apply in a special way to Father John Mary Vianney. For it is not beautiful and eloquent words that convert, but examples of virtue and of a powerful love of God.

The Curé's Style

As long as the Curé of Ars was still able to write his sermons, he devoted the greatest care to this work. He wrote with ease, to judge from the absence of scratched-out words in his manuscripts. But he did much copying from his favorite authors, and felt no scruples about it. He sometimes took entire pages from collections of sermons, but usually he changed a word, an expression here and there, or a term he considered too pedantic, using instead one better suited to the capacities of his audience.

It was because his sermons were not his original composition and because his memory was very poor that he had considerable difficulty learning them by heart. He found writing easy compared to the task of learning a sermon and delivering it without making any mistakes.

He devoted a good portion of each week to preparing and learning his Sunday sermon. One thing is certain. He always made use of models deserving his highest trust. He often reproduced their doctrine word for word because he came to realize, as his fame grew, that he was usually "under close surveillance" by some of his colleagues. There was a tendency among some of the clergy to think he must be either a visionary or a charlatan. After all, everyone knew this young priest was reputed to be ignorant, and had been dismissed from the seminary for incompetence. Yet now he had become very successful in the confessional, was sought after as a spiritual director, and even claimed to have been in personal combat with the devil. He was actually denounced at the

Archbishopric of Belley in 1823, when the parish of Ars was separated from the Archdiocese of Lyons.

The reason Father Vianney was subjected to such severe criticism can be found in his condemnation of the moral evils prevalent in his parish.

Jansenism

Some have accused the Curé of Ars of Jansenism. That is surely a mistake. If we look through a list of the books in his small library, we will not find a single Jansenistic book. Besides, Jansenism was a heresy on the subject of grace and on man's cooperation with God. In practice, Jansenism was a form of rigorism that alienated the laity from the frequent practice of Communion and from strong devotion to the Blessed Virgin Mary.

Now, on all three points, the doctrine and practice of John Mary Vianney were at opposite poles from Jansenism. No one ever trusted in God's grace more than he. No one ever preached with such fire on the need of freely cooperating with this grace. No one ever urged more than he the frequent reception of Holy Communion by those who were worthy.

The fact remains that he was a man of his time. A certain austerity characterized preaching and moral teaching. He was under obligation to conform to the spirit of his age or be subject to official rebukes on the part of ecclesiastical authorities. When, on the other hand, he felt he had the support of his bishop, he softened his language. He knew his bishop was on his side when the prelate silenced his detractors with these explicit words:

"Gentlemen, I don't know whether the Curé of Ars is a learned man, but I do know that he is a very enlightened man."

It must be admitted that none of his other writings have come down to us except the texts of his catechism classes. These were not written by him but recorded by some of his hearers.

We should add that John Vianney put little stock in his own private inspirations and ideas. He was always ready to consult one of his colleagues in cases he found too difficult to solve himself.

An Example of the Curé's Manner

In closing this brief account of our saint's mode of preaching, we would like to offer at least one concrete example of it.

As we know, his parish suffered from two serious moral evils: too many taverns and a craze for dancing.

He did not relax his attack on the taverns until he had forced them to close their doors. His biographer, Abbé Trochu, has pointed out that in this matter he followed the guidance of a sermonary published in 1739 by Joseph Lambert, a doctor from the Sorbonne. This book was entitled: *La Manière de bien instruire les pauvres et en particulier les gens des campagnes*...(The manner of instructing the poor and especially the people of the rural areas).

When we compare his own sermons with this book we realize that he had read it, followed its advice, and often copied it verbatim.

The same holds true in the matter of the dance. However, in the case of the dancing craze in Ars, we find some of his own reflections which reveal his caustic spirit. Even if he was a man who had been unable to pass the examinations at the seminary, he proved in this instance that on occasion he knew how to use biting sarcasm. Here, for example, is a passage from one of his sermons condemning dancing, which was obviously written tongue in cheek.

"One day I happened to be passing in front of a great fire. I took a handful of very dry straw. I threw it into the fire, telling it not to burn. Those who witnessed this action said to me mockingly: 'You are wasting your time telling the straw not to burn, that won't stop it from burning.'

"'And how is that?' I answered, 'since I told it not to burn?'

"What do you think about it, good mother?... Isn't that what you told your daughter: to be a very good girl, when you gave her permission to go to the dance?..."

On this subject, he never grew tired. His penetrating voice, which was midway between a nasal twang and a tenor, bored into the ears of his audience like a drill:

"The Devil surrounds a dance the way a wall surrounds a garden."

"Dancing is the rope by which the Devil drags most souls to hell."

"Everyone who enters a ball leaves his guardian angel at the door, and a devil takes his place. And so very soon there are as many devils as dancers in the ballroom."

Of course, he said all these things only out of his great love for the souls of his hearers, out of his overriding horror of sexual impurity, and a powerful desire to see the spirit of Jesus Christ and of His Gospel rule the hearts of all his parishioners.

On one occasion he gave the fiddler hired to play at one of the dances twice the sum he was about to earn on condition that he leave without playing his instrument.

In the end the little pastor had the last word. He brought about the reign of the Gospel in his parish.

A Parish Transformed

Rapid Changes

We now know the means the young Curé of Ars used to conquer his parish for Jesus Christ. The supernatural means of prayer and penance practiced to the point of heroism. Likewise, natural means that were carefully "supernaturalized" by his intention: visits to his parishioners, sermons, the example of his own life, and his liberal almsgiving to the poor even when he had to strip himself of necessities.

Such were his weapons of war.

And what were the results?

When we consider that the transformation of a parish is usually very slow and painful even in the most favorable circumstances, then we can say that the results obtained by the Curé of Ars were truly amazing.

Abbé Vianney had been at Ars slightly more than two years when the rumor spread that he was being transferred to Salles-en-Beaujolais. On hearing the news, a deacon at the Seminary *Saint-Irénée* wrote to his benefactress, Mlle. d'Ars:

"I learned with great sorrow and surprise that you have lost your holy pastor. Providence had given him to the parish to make godliness flourish there. I pray with all my heart that he will be succeeded by a priest who is able to maintain the fervor that now reigns at Ars."

So we see the religious climate of Ars was already profoundly changed. What a turnabout! Before Abbé Vianney arrived in Ars, no one would have thought of using the word "fervor" to describe this disintegrating parish.

We also have testimony from the Curé himself. On November 7, 1823, he wrote to his old friend *"Mère Fayot"* at Les Robins, and did not hesitate to say quite frankly:

"I am in a little parish that is filled with religious spirit, that serves the good God with all its heart."

Can we not detect a shout of victory in these words?

A few months before writing these words the Curé of Ars had organized a parish pilgrimage to Notre Dame de Fourvière, in Lyons. It had been the center of many pilgrimages before the French Revolution. The young pastor naturally hoped to be able to revive the piety of "Old France" among his parishioners, as he had known it as a child and even more as a student at Ecully.

We have a vivid picture of the valiant efforts to restore religious fervor throughout France by means of preached missions. Everywhere there was intense activity to overcome the ravages of the French Revolution and bring the people back to their great national traditions, to what has rightly been called "the vocation of France."

The parish of Ars had hastened to respond to its pastor's appeal to take part in the pilgrimage of Fourvière. It took place on August 6, 1823, the feast of the parish's patron saint, St. Sixtus. The pilgrims started out about midnight, and did not return until the evening of the following day.

We can surmise the intense prayers the young pastor offered to the Blessed Virgin Mary, entrusting his parishioners to her protection.

Once the trend was started, it continued to gain momentum. During the Jubilee year of 1826, Abbé Vianney preached many sermons not only in his own parish but in all the neighboring parishes where he had been invited both as preacher and confessor. A new impetus had been given to religious conversion and spiritual fervor. In 1827, the Curé of Ars had the chance to give his parishioners one of those missions which brought blessings on the entire countryside.

It can be said that the 1827 mission sealed the spiritual conquest of Ars.

Catherine Lassagne was one of the Curé's most active helpers, and was to be at his side through the remaining years of his life. Referring to the conversion of Ars in 1827, she wrote:

"There had been a revolution in the people's hearts.... God's grace was so powerful that very few could resist it.... Almost everybody was striving mightily to overcome the forces of evil and sin. Human respect was cast aside. Everyone would have been ashamed not to do good and not to practice his religion. People appeared to be serious and thoughtful. Some of them who had not been to confession in many years were heard to say aloud on the roads: 'I want to go to confession!' Everyone seemed to be eager to do the right thing. *Monsieur le Curé* said to them after one of his instructions: "My brothers, *Ars isn't Ars any more!* I have heard confessions and preached during jubilees and missions. I have never come upon anything like this."

The trend to conversion and renewal was not merely a participation in the great missionary movement that was unfolding over the entire Kingdom of France. Ars was what might be called "an islet of holiness."

What do we mean by "an islet of holiness"?

For one thing, the faithful came from all sides on Sundays and feastdays to attend Mass with devotion, as well as vespers, the recitation of rosary, and Abbé Vianney's catechism classes. But that was not all. They came on weekdays, too, and this showed how profound the spiritual renewal of Ars really was.

France would be fortunate if it could witness once again such a love of prayer as occurred in Ars in the early 1800's. It was not unusual to see a young farmer leading his yoke of oxen out to the fields, quietly "telling" his beads. Every night the churchbells would peel out, calling to prayer. Those who could come would go to the church for evening prayers. Those who couldn't would gather in their homes around a religious picture, and pray as a family. Peace and joy reigned in the little parish. Out in the fields hymns would resound from field to field, as the farmers plowed their land. Oaths and blasphemous words were things of the past. A pilgrim from Lyons told how amazed he was to see several peasants busy lifting up a horse that had fallen into a ditch. They showed no signs of anger, neither striking the poor animal nor shouting uncouth words at it.

In the homes of Ars, grace was now recited before and after meals, in French. At the sound of the *Angelus* all work stopped. People would fall to their knees wherever they were and pray. Beyond that, the young pastor had taught his parishioners to "bless the hours." This consisted in reciting a *Hail Mary* whenever the clock in the church steeple rang out the hours. Actually, the clock had been specially installed by Abbé Vianney, with a clearly readable dial. Many of the parishioners joined their pastor in this ancient custom which many of them had learned as children before the Revolution.

Another ancient custom had been revived in many French parishes. It was the blessing of little wooden crosses each year on the feast of the Finding of the Holy Cross, May 3rd. The peasants made the crosses themselves and brought them to the parish church to be blessed. After this ceremony and the Mass that followed, the crosses were planted out in the fields, where they remained until harvest time. When the farmers came upon them as they reaped their wheat and barley, they would kneel down on the earth and recite the *Lord's Prayer* or a *Hail Mary*. The Curé of Ars had restored this ancient custom in his parish.

Sometimes the peasants of the neighboring villages made fun of the good example of Ars.

"If you listen to your Curé," they would say mockingly, "he'll make Capuchin Friars out of you."

"Our pastor is a saint," they would retort, "and we feel we must obey him."

Monsignor Convert came to know many of the descendants of families that had known the saint personally. He was appointed pastor to Ars in July, 1889, and remained at this post many years. He heard many stories of the way Father Vianney's parishioners followed his counsels on piety and the practice of the Christian virtues. They still seemed to reflect some of the spiritual fervor of the past. It was as if they had received the visible imprint of their beloved pastor.

To quote Msgr. Convert:

"Their faces bore an imprint of holiness that we have rarely noticed elsewhere in the same degree. A serenity, a sort of radiant blessedness made them stand out among thousands."

The inhabitants of Ars were soon renowned for their proverbial honesty. Before the coming of Father Vianney they had acted "like everyone else." In other words, they had had no scruples about selling rancid butter and claiming it was fresh, or selling incubated eggs. They readily sought ways of hiding the flaws in their livestock at the market. They had no great respect for the property rights of others. All that mattered was not getting caught. No one had any qualms about pilfering fruit, fodder, and turnips from his neighbor's fields.

But once Ars had regained its Christian spirit, such behavior was abhorred. Benedict Trève has related that as a child he had dared to take a pear from the stand of a fruit-vendor. When he started to eat it at home, his mother asked him sternly where he had gotten it. He was obliged to tell. Without a moment's hesitation the mother tied her son's hands behind his back and took him back to the fruit-vendor's stand, whipping him all the way. Only then did she untie him. He returned the pear and asked the vendor's pardon.

We could go on and on, giving examples of the moral and spiritual renewal in the parish. Among the most beautiful expressions of Catholic faith were the colorful ceremonies for the greatest feast-days of the year, such as the Feast of Corpus Christi, with its magnificent procession, with the altar adorned with countless flowers, and with the army of choirboys preceding the canopy under which Father Vianney was carrying the monstrance. We shall describe all this more fully later.

The Curé of Ars and the Schools

The Church of France has often been accused of encouraging *ignorantism*, of showing no interest in the education of the common people, and of being hostile to the advancement of science.

A man like John Mary Vianney who was not an eagle from the intellectual point of view might understandably have tended to neglect the education of his people. At that period of French history elementary education was not yet obligatory. Since the

French Revolution, the schools had not yet regained the ground lost when all the religious congregations of teaching Sisters and Brothers had been dispersed. After the restoration of religion by the Concordat of 1801, the school system was gradually rebuilt both by the members of the old religious communities and by members of new congregations. The State had all but destroyed France's schools, but had as yet accomplished almost nothing to restore the educational system.

The story was no different for Ars, in the Department of Ain. Statistics for this Department for the year 1830 show the following figures: communes without schools numbered 175. In the entire Department there were 452 primary schools, attended by 11,824 boys and 6,687 girls. Thus, there were a total of 18,511 children in the schools out of a total population of 346,000. As there were over 10,000 births per year, it is easy to calculate that only a very small percentage of the children of school age received even a very limited education.

Ars was among the communes without a school when Father Vianney arrived in 1818. To be sure, during the winter a teacher was brought in from the outside to give classes to groups of boys and girls together. The young pastor considered this system not only inadequate, but dangerous. And so he decided to establish a school for girls, in order to avoid what we now call "co-ed" education.

Starting a girls' school was no easy undertaking for a village pastor who had no money of his own. He had to begin by finding a site and some women teachers. It occurred to him to train two of his most promising young women parishioners for this task. First, there was Catherine Lassagne, who was to play a very important role in the Curé's life. The other young woman was Benoîte Lardet.

Catherine Lassagne was exactly twenty years younger than Father Vianney. Her mother was a devout woman named Claudine, who had been one of the first to return to the fervent customs of the past.

Early in 1823, Catherine, who was then 17, and her friend Benoîte were sent to be instructed by the Sisters of St. Joseph at Fareins. Father Vianney paid for their board. They completed their studies and began to tutor the children of Fareins.

This novitiate or normal school training continued for a year and a half. Every Sunday our young girls returned to Ars, thus remaining in intimate contact with the parish.

In November, 1824, the free private school for girls opened at Ars in a building which Father Vianney had bought for 2,400 francs, but which would now be worth more than a million. In addition to Catherine and Benoîte, a third young woman shared in running the school. This was Jeanne Marie Chanay, who came from Jassans and was a few years older than the other two. Having less education than the others, Jeanne Marie was to become the housekeeper, cook, baker, and laundress of the small community.

The Curé of Ars did not intend for his three teachers to be Sisters in the strict sense. He did not require them to wear a religious habit, take vows, or follow a written rule. It was enough, from his point of view, that they were exemplary Christian women. Catherine Lassagne was the guiding spirit of the group. She was to have much to suffer from Jeanne Marie's gruff temperament. Her beloved companion Benoîte died prematurely in 1830, and was replaced by Marie Filliat who came from Misérieux. A Godfearing girl to be sure, but imperious and hard to get along with. She proved to be one more cross for Catherine to endure with patience and charity.

From the start, the school was a great success, perhaps too great a success. For the small building in which it was located was very soon overcrowded. As no tuition was charged by the school, which was rare at that time, parents brought their children from neighboring villages — Savigneux, Misérieux, Villeneuve, etc. And as the little girls could not go home every night, a way was found to provide lodging for them. The Curé's intention had been to found a day school, but somehow it had turned into a boarding school. Even so, no money was required of the parents. They simply furnished the beds and bedclothes. They also brought supplies of food whenever they could.

Soon a profound change occurred in the institution. In his charity, the Curé could not see why education should be restricted to persons of means. He decided to open a shelter for little orphan girls and for the daughters of the very poor. And so one Sunday morning in 1827, he unveiled his plan to his parishioners, asking them to pray that he might do God's will in the matter. First of all, the school would have to be enlarged. He bought a piece of property and started building. As an incentive to his parishioners, he set to work helping the masons, the carpenters, and the roofers.

Next, he decided to stop accepting boarders from the neighboring villages after October, 1827. The school would be only for day students from Ars, as originally planned. Thus, the boarding school would be reserved for orphans from eight to twelve years old, as well as for a few older girls ranging from fifteen to twenty.

Father Vianney gave the newly organized institution the beautiful name of *La Providence*, and the name stayed with it.

La Providence

La Providence of Ars played a tremendous role in the life of our saint. He was truly the father of all the children and adolescents who came there. He was also the father of their devoted teachers. He used to spend most of his free time there, while he still had time to spare. It was here he ate his meals, if such may be called the few minutes he spent in what he called "feeding his cadaver."

However *La Providence* meant a great deal more to him than a place to eat and to visit. As he saw it, *La Providence* was a powerhouse of prayer and supplication. He called upon his little girls to pray for all the intentions dear to his heart. He brought to them his anxiety over the spiritual welfare of the poor sinners who came to him.

This is the way Catherine Lassagne described his relationship with the children of *La Providence:*

"*Monsieur le Curé* used to cultivate their souls. He came every day to teach catechism in his house of Providence. Heaven's graces, won by his prayers, accompanied his words. These poor children, especially the older girls, were amazed they had taken so long to understand their religion and their obligations. Almost all of them wanted to make a general confession to him. These confessions lasted quite a while. Father Vianney never hurried them, because they learned more as they went on. And these poor children were completely transformed. They were no longer little scatterbrains, but fervent young Christians who would persevere in the path of goodness. A number of them became Sisters, others were to be good mothers of large families, and still others became domestic servants. Very, very few failed to persevere.

"I have heard *Monsieur le Curé* say that only on judgment day would the good accomplished in that house finally be revealed."

We might point out that ten years before his death, Father Vianney was obliged to give up the supervision and even the ownership of his favorite charitable work. This was a very great sacrifice for him.

The Academy criticized *La Providence* because of the overcrowding of pupils. For sometimes sixty or more children were crowded together in space intended for only twenty or thirty. Besides, some of the families of Ars complained that their daughters were mixing with uneducated orphan girls who had been picked up on the highways! For these reasons the Bishop of Belley asked the Curé of Ars in 1849 to turn over his school together with all its annexes and property to a religious congregation, the Sisters of St. Joseph of Bourg.

Although Catherine Lassagne did not speak of her own loss, she spoke of the Curé's:

"It was a great sacrifice for him, because after he had turned everything over, he felt he could not and should not interfere in the affairs of others. He completely withdrew from it. Several children were kept on for a short time, then they were sent away. The children of the parish, that is, the little girls, continued to be given free schooling."

A little later, when we talk about the miracles St. John Mary Vianney worked during his lifetime, we shall speak of *La Providence* again.

The Catechism Classes

Among the unforeseen results of the foundation of *La Providence* were the famous catechism classes of Ars.

As we have mentioned, the holy pastor came every day to the school to teach Christian doctrine to the children. This went on from All Saints' Day, November 1st, until the great day of the First Holy Communion. The Curé began by catechizing the little boys at the church. In those days, everyone in France used to get up very early. This boys' catechism class was held at six o'clock in the morning.

The catechetical instruction for the girls was given only at the end of the regular classes, around eleven o'clock. The school day closed with the recitation of the "Litany of Divine Providence." At the last words of the litany, the pastor would enter very quietly and begin his catechism lesson.

At first, only the children and their teachers were present for the lesson. But after the village of Ars became a pilgrimage center for all of France and even foreign lands, the pilgrims who had come to see the Curé would gather near the doors of the school to wait for him. Then little by little they began slipping into the classroom and listening to the lessons given to the students. This practice became so popular that in time the school could not hold them all, and the catechism classes had to be given in the church. This change took place in 1845. From that time until his death in 1859 the Curé of Ars taught his catechism class at eleven o'clock in the morning before a large audience, which at various times included famous men, church prelates, and renowned preachers.

Gradually Abbé Vianney adopted a less informal tone in his catechism lessons, but continued to illustrate them with edifying stories he had been storing in his memory since childhood about the lives of the saints. Interestingly enough, although he had great trouble remembering almost everything else, he easily remembered countless details from his reading on the saints. His catechism lessons were really little sermons. The fire of his love of God shone through his words.

When the Curé gave his catechetical instructions in the church, he had such an intense awareness of God's presence in the Blessed Sacrament that he could never get himself to talk with his back to the tabernacle. And so he had a lectern installed on the right side of the sanctuary. From this pulpit of sorts he spoke without constraint, but his awareness of Christ's presence in the Blessed Sacrament often caused his voice to tremble.

We shall talk at greater length about John Vianney's love of the Eucharistic Christ when we discuss his spirituality.

The Boys' School

Let no one think that the Curé of Ars had no interest in the boys' school. The co-educational school that had existed in Ars in 1818 before the girls' school was opened had continued to function after 1823 as a boys' school. It seems that soon afterward a resident public-school teacher was assigned to Ars.

Catherine Lassagne has written about it as follows:

"*Monsieur le Curé* wanted a God-fearing and reputable teacher for the boys until such time as someone from the parish had been properly trained to take in the responsibility. Then he established a foundation for the Brothers of the Holy Family. This took place after he had turned over his *Providence* to the Sisters of St. Joseph, and the Brothers came in 1850."

Actually, the Brothers arrived in Ars on March 10, 1849. The public school teacher who filled the breach was John Pertinand, and he became one of the Curé's best friends and co-workers. After the saint's death, he was among the principal witnesses on behalf of his beatification.

The Parish of Ars is Beautified

Together with the spiritual transformation of the parish came a continual effort on the part of its pastor to beautify the church and everything pertaining to divine worship.

By a royal decree of June 20, 1821, Ars was raised from the rank of a mission attached to the parish of Misérieux to the status of an independent parish.

Father Vianney was already busy renovating his shabby and dilapidated church, which was now also too small. The belfry was made of wood, and when its bells were rung, it used to sway back and forth with them. The bells were no longer rung long and loud lest the bell tower collapse and fall into the neighboring cemetery. During the month of August, 1819, at the Curé's repeated requests, the mayor started repairs on the belfry. This time, it was constructed of solid red brick, on a square plan. Twin windows of Romanesque style gave it a graceful appearance. As soon as the repairs were completed, Abbé Vianney gave the church a second bell, which he named the "Bell of the Holy Rosary."

To enlarge the church he undertook the construction of several chapels over the years, and they can still be seen today. Before his time, the church had consisted only of a nave.

Catherine Lassagne has given explicit details about these activities:

"(After the construction of the bell tower) he had the chapel of the Blessed Virgin built—it was blessed on August 6, 1820—and later the chapel of St. John the Baptist (in 1823), then the chapel of St. Philomena (before 1836), and the chapels of the Holy Angels and of the Passion. All these chapels cost him a great deal of money. He did not ask his parishioners to help him, and did not take up a collection. I don't know whether he made special requests of rich people, and nobody worried about the expenses.... Providence always came to his assistance, and he always paid his debts."

Besides, Catherine also tells us that he had "wainscotting installed all around his church," and he himself did the painting.

He added many statues and pictures. It was his view that pictures were very useful for most ordinary Christians:

"Sometimes the sight of a picture is enough to touch us and to convert us. Often pictures make as strong an impression on us as the things they represent."

But the Curé's greatest concern was to obtain the most beautiful vestments and vessels possible for the celebration of the sacred liturgy. To his mind, nothing could be too beautiful for the main altar, for the tabernacle, for all the surrounding objects, and for the liturgical vestments the priest uses to celebrate the Eucharistic Sacrifice.

He found an eminent benefactor who held the same views. Through the years his generous gifts brought Father Vianney great consolations amid his trials and worries.

This benefactor was Viscount Francis Garnier des Garets d'Ars, the brother of Mademoiselle d'Ars, the local chatelaine. He lived in Paris, but often visited with his family at the château. In the summer of 1819 he met the new pastor of Ars, and was conquered. From that time on, he always spoke of the "zealous and respectable Curé" in his letters to his sister. He did much more. He declared:

"The village sanctuary will never be as sumptuous and magnificent as I would like it to be."

These words were written in a letter dated October 18, 1822. He immediately put in orders with the most reputed artisans of Paris. On May 5, 1823,.he announced he was sending three banners embroidered in silver. Then, he sent vestments of silk and gold cloth for use on feastdays, and a black velvet vestment with red braid for Good Friday. He promised to provide a canopy for the Blessed Sacrament, to enhance the processions for the Feast of Corpus Christi, the Body and Blood of Christ.

Through a fortunate error, when the canopy arrived it was too large to go through the church door. The Viscount did not hesitate to have the facade remodeled, so that it would have a large doorway worthy of renovated structure. It was after these repairs that the two ramps and the porch were added that can still be seen in front of the church of Ars.

We cannot tell the whole story here. Suffice it to say that the Viscount continued to give lavishly as long as there was need. The pastor was so happy when the crates arrived that he would call out to passers-by to come and admire their contents. Laughing and crying at once like a child, he would comment:

"In heaven, everything will be even more beautiful!"

Great Trials -
Great Victories

All Great Saints Endure Great Trials

There is a law that has been forcefully set forth by all masters of the spiritual life, and it is this: there is no way to attain a high degree of perfection except through great trials. There never has been and never will be any easy path to sanctity.

We have good reason to refer to our earthly pilgrimage toward God as an ascent. The highest peaks are surrounded by precipices. We cannot reach the top without exhausting effort and encountering great perils.

Great saints must go through great trials. It is almost as if we said: great generals must fight great battles, great statesmen must accomplish great political reforms.

St. John Mary Vianney was no exception to this rule. In this chapter we shall touch on his most terrible trials as well as his greatest consolations. St. Teresa of Avila and St. John of the Cross agree in teaching that in the spiritual life there tend to be alternating times of trial and consolation. Even Mary the Mother of God, the most privileged of creatures, had a sword pierce her heart. Obviously, her trials were as unique and incomparable as her holiness. What sorrow can compare with hers? To see her Son die on a cross of shame and yet be unable to die with him!

What we are about to relate is not a series of anecdotes, but events of deep spiritual significance, and sufferings that were permitted by God in order to fashion a man into a saint.

Terrible Calumnies

We shall begin by talking of trials on the part of men. This is not to say that the Devil had no part in the abominable machinations against the young Curé of Ars, but simply that he was making use of human instruments.

In the last chapter we spoke of the holy virulence with which John Mary Vianney tongue-lashed the vices and misconduct that were such a blot on his parish. Dancing, in particular, but also drunkenness.

It was inevitable that all whose interest had been jeopardized by his interdictions were soon up-in-arms against him. The tavern-keepers, the heavy drinkers, the profaners of the Lord's day, the patrons of the public dances—all felt they had been attacked in their most private preserves, their passions, their bad habits, their sensual appetites.

Within the precincts of the parish, no one dared to go beyond the stage of quiet grumbling. They said their pastor was too strict, and they would continue to say it for a long time to come. But in any event, they obeyed him. They acknowledged he was a holy man. So those who were against the Curé had to confront his friends who supported him.

However, some delinquent youths outside the parish did not hesitate to use the loathsome weapon of calumny against him. They pointed to this man who lived a truly angelic life, flogged his body to subdue it and make of it a docile servant of God, who lived only to love Jesus Christ and bring others to love Him, and accused him of secret debauchery. In proof of this they pointed to his emaciated frame, to the pallor of his face. They composed obscene songs about him, wrote him anonymous letters, and posted disgusting and insulting signs on his door.

In the words of Catherine Lassagne, "during that period he was calumniated, mocked. They would play the trumpet under his window and send him insulting letters. He was not terrified by all that. He simply continued to pray, to work for the salvation of souls, never complaining and following a most austere rule of life. In later years he said that the time when he was persecuted had been the best time of his life."

This is not to say that all these attacks did not hurt his feelings. For by nature he was very sensitive and quick. Without the high degree of virtue he had already attained he could easily have given vent to anger and pique. But he had learned to control his emotions. Here is one example given us by Catherine Lassagne:

"This I have been told by someone in whom he confided. Soon after he came to Ars, a young man entered the rectory and began hurling abuses at him. He listened quietly without answering, accompanied his visitor into the courtyard, and embraced him. But the effort he had made to control his temper made itself felt almost at once. By the time he returned to his room he found that his whole body was covered with pimples."

His heroic patience was put to the sternest and most humiliating test. He was denounced to his new bishop, who had been appointed to the restored see of Belley in 1823. Bishop Devie decided there should be an inquiry into the matter, and entrusted it to the dean of Trevoux. We do not know what transpired, but it is clear that the saintly young pastor was made to suffer cruelly. In later years he reportedly said:

"If I had known when I arrived in Ars all that I would have to suffer there, I would have died on the spot."

The idea came to him that he should leave his parish. One of the witnesses at his beatification process has told about it:

"He was so tired of all the evil rumors that people were spreading about him that he wanted to leave his parish. Indeed, he would have done so if someone had not come to him and convinced him that his departure could appear to confirm these sordid attacks."

What, then, should he do? He abandoned himself to God's mercy. He refused to break his silence. He did good to all those who, he knew, wished him harm. He never stopped saying to his friends: "We must pray for them." When another priest complained to him that he was similarly persecuted, he answered:

"Do as I do. I let them say everything they wanted and in this way they finally stopped talking."

Nevertheless, he expected the worst. In February, 1843, he said:

"I thought a time would come when I would be driven out of Ars with cudgels, or that His Excellency would have me removed by an interdict, and then I would end my days in the prisons...." By way of conclusion, he said: "I see that I do not deserve such a great favor from heaven."

Frontal Attacks

No, the Devil must have had some part of these early trials. But the day soon came when he began to make frontal attacks himself on the Curé of Ars, as he had once done to Job, the man of God of the Old Testament.

The incidents of "devilry" we are about to recount are not open to doubt. They have been attested to by unimpeachable witnesses, and related by all of the saint's biographers.

The diabolic persecutions lasted about thirty-five years, from 1824 to 1858. They coincided with violent temptations to despair. Like other great saints, John Mary Vianney came to believe he was destined to go to hell. Deep within him he seemed to hear a terrifying voice saying:

"The time has come to sink into hell!"

However, that was only a cruel temptation. To help us understand what is to follow, let us remember that theologians distinguish degrees of diabolic action upon human beings. First, by way of *temptation,* and no one escapes this. Secondly, by way of *infestation,* a rare phenomenon that occurred extensively in our saint's life. Then come *external* and *internal obsessions,* and finally *diabolic possession.*

Perhaps the most useful thing to do here is to cite at length a passage from Catherine Lassagne's memoirs concerning John Mary Vianney's battles against diabolic forces.

A Page from Catherine Lassagne's Memoirs

"During the year when *Monsieur le Curé* was preparing to found a school for girls—I think it was about 1824—we were at Fareins, Benoîte Lardet and I, at the Sisters of St. Joseph, for our teachers' training. We used to come home every Saturday from Fareins to spend Sunday at Ars. One day I was told that

Monsieur le Curé was very much disturbed by certain noises he heard during the night around his rectory. We thought it must be thieves or someone who wanted to harm him."

Note how this story ties in with the preceding one. The poor pastor was being showered with insults and threats. He had good reason to think someone wanted to kill him. Inasmuch as he was not at all inclined to be gullible and superstitious, it never crossed his mind at the start that the Devil could have anything to do with it.

Catherine Lassagne continues:

"Soon several young men armed themselves with guns to protect *Monsieur le Curé*. Some stood guard in the belfry, the others stayed in the rectory.

"One youth named Verchère was in the room next to *Monsieur le Curé's,* when all of a sudden during the night he heard a terrible noise. It seemed as though someone was tearing to pieces a large wardrobe that stood in the same room. The poor young man was terrified and ran in haste toward Father Vianney, calling out to him. As the holy pastor told about it later: 'My poor Verchère had forgotten he had a gun, he thought he was lost!'"

It is worth mentioning that this same André Verchère, who died in Ars in 1879, gave two depositions at the saint's beatification process, and his testimony confirms what we have just related on every count.

It was he who had said to his pastor:

"I think it's the Devil!"

He closed his testimony with these words:

"When the noise stopped, we went back to bed. *Monsieur le Curé* came to me again the following night, and asked me to return with him. I answered: '*Monsieur le Curé*, I've had enough of all that!'"

Father Vianney refused to acknowledge right away that it was really the Devil after all. At first, he looked for natural explanations. To quote Catherine Lassagne again:

"In the beginning, the holy *Curé* had armed himself with an iron pitchfork, which he set beside his bed. For he said he could hear the curtains of his bed tearing, and expected to find them in shreds in the morning. At such moments he would pick up his pitchfork, imagining at first that he had an infestation of rats. But the more he shook, the louder the ripping sounds became. The next morning, he discovered the curtains had not been torn at all.

"One night after a heavy snow, there were shouts in the rectory courtyard. The next day, there were no footprints of any kind to be seen. Father Vianney then realized he did not have robbers prowling around his rectory and disturbing his sleep. So he sent away his guards and remained to fight alone."

From the moment Father Vianney realized with whom he had to deal, he prepared for battle with holy vigor. We know from his own admissions what went on. Catherine Lassagne has related:

"We heard from his own lips about various attacks he experienced on the part of the spirit of darkness. The Devil used to knock at the door of his room and call out in a shrill voice: 'Vianney! Vianney!'

"'The *Grappin* knocked on my door last night,' he would say. [*Grappin* was his nickname for the Devil.] 'I didn't tell him to come in, but he came in anyway. He banged a general alarm on the water pitcher on the mantel. He has banged on it very often.'

"'Another time,' he continued, 'it seemed as if there were a large horse in the room below, jumping to the ceiling and then falling back onto the tile floor on his four hoofs.'

"He said that on several occasions he heard an army of Austrians, of Cossacks in his courtyard, talking confusedly a language he did not understand.

"One day he said to me: 'Don't put the straw into my bed, because if there is too much the Devil will throw me on the floor.' I understood that if his straw mat was a little fuller, instead of remaining in the middle of the bed, he would stay on one side, almost on the boards as he usually did. In such a position, it would be easy for the Devil to make him slide to the floor.

"Another time, he said: '*Grappin* came last night. He placed himself under my head like a very soft and comfortable bolster. He kept uttering plaintive cries like a sick man at death's door.'

"Once when he was busy reading or reciting his breviary by his fireside, he heard a noise as if someone were blowing hard and vomiting gravel or grains of wheat. Assuming it was the Devil, he said: 'I shall go over to *La Providence*; I shall tell what you are doing, so they will despise you.' And he did come over and tell us about it. The Devil had stopped at once."

This passage shows us the tactics of our holy priest in his long duel with the Devil. He had finally gotten used to the attacks of the Devil, or as he called him, *Grappin*. He spoke to him as to a fellow traveller. Above all, he treated him with scorn.

This approach was also used by the famous priest of the Oratory, Charles de Condren, who did not favor the great public demonstrations used by the exorcists of his time. Instead, he preferred to treat the Devil with scorn, and thus obtained better results than everyone else.

What we must remember of all that has so far been said is that the Devil frequently and one might say habitually interfered in St. John Mary Vianney's life. His activities took on a great variety of forms.

To quote Catherine Lassagne once more, "On other occasions it seemed to Father Vianney as if someone came up the stairs to his room with heavy boots, and then stood in front of him. Yet he could see no one.

"The Devil's nocturnal visits were frequent. They occurred above all, according to the words of the servant of God, when there were sinners eager to be converted. Usually these persons would arrive at Ars shortly afterwards, to set their consciences in order and to start a better life, all of which did not please the Devil at all.

Some may be inclined to think these were merely harmless pranks on the part of the *Grappin*. The truth of the matter is that such an explanation does not correspond to the Devil's character, or to his nature as an extremely intelligent and powerful spirit. Fortunately for us, the Devil can use his power and intellect only to the extent that God permits him to. We should also remember that we are not alone in our struggle against him. Father Vianney, in particular, derived invincible supernatural strength from prayer and by invoking his Guardian Angel as well as the Blessed Virgin Mary.

Disbelief

There was so much talk about all these happenings that the saint's fellow priests soon learned about them. Most of them thought it was a big joke. This time, they thought, it is altogether evident that he is losing his mind. His excessive privations and penances have unbalanced him.

We really cannot blame these sober-minded priests for coming to such a conclusion. And they did not hesitate to tell Father Vianney exactly what they thought of him, as we see from the following incident.

It happened during the year 1826. The Roman Jubilee of 1825 had been extended to the entire Church, and was being preached in all the parishes of France. The priests in the Diocese of Belley would gather to celebrate the Jubilee in one parish and then in another.

One morning in December, 1826, the Curé of Ars went on foot to Saint-Trivier-sur-Moignans to preach the Jubilee. As he walked along, he recited his rosary as he had always done. Now, the region of Dombes through which he was passing had many more ponds and marshes then than in our own day. During summer evenings the lights of the will-o'-the-wisp were often seen above the bogs, but never in December. And yet that December morning Father Vianney could see sinister gleams of light everywhere he looked. The air seemed to be aflame. On each side of the road the bushes seemed to be burning.

All along the eight-mile walk Father Vianney had the feeling that Satan was following him, seeking to prevent him from carrying out the task he had accepted in honor of the Jubilee.

At Saint-Trivier, unusual sounds were heard every night in the rectory where Father Vianney and several other priests were staying. The sounds seemed to be coming from the room occupied by Father Vianney. And so his colleagues complained to him that he was making too much noise.

"It's the *Grappin*," he replied with his usual frankness. And he added: "He is furious about the good that is being accomplished here."

The Curé's fellow-priests just laughed at him. One of them even took the opportunity to say:

"You don't eat, you don't sleep. It's all in your head. You have rats running around in your brain!"

He might easily have answered: "If all this is going on inside my head, how is it that you are hearing so much noise?" But with his usual humility, he said nothing.

The next night, a noise was heard outside like the rumbling of a heavily-loaded carriage that made the rectory shake. It almost seemed as though the house would collapse, as had happened in 1820 to the rectory of a neighboring village, as the result of a heavy wind. Everyone awoke in a state of panic. Among those present were Father Grangier, the local pastor, Father Benoîte, his curate, and Father Chevalon, a diocesan missionary. The housekeeper also arose, wondering what was going on. At that very moment there was such an uproar in the Curé of Ars' room that they all cried out at once:

"He's being killed!"

They rushed into his room, and found Father Vianney sleeping peacefully. And yet it was evident his bed had been dragged out into the middle of the room.

By this time Father Vianney was awake. Without any show of emotion, he told them:

"The *Grappin* dragged me out like that and made all that commotion. It's nothing, really.... I am very sorry I didn't warn you. But it's a good sign: we'll catch a *big fish* tomorrow."

However, the next day nothing unusual happened until evening. Then Monsieur des Murs arrived, a nobleman who had long neglected his religious obligations as was common practice among those of his social class. He was coming to confess his sins to Father Vianney. His example made a profound impression on everyone.

Catherine Lassagne concluded: "But after that no one dared to make jokes about it any more. Instead, they said: 'The Curé of Ars is a saint,' and they held him in respect from that time on."

Exorcisms

News quickly spread to distant places about the Curé of Ars' encounters with the Devil, how he scorned the *Grappin*, and spoke to him with magnificent authority in the name of our Lord Jesus Christ. As a result, many came to him to ask for his help in cases of diabolic possession. Bishop Devie authorized him to use his powers as an exorcist whenever the circumstances required.

Among all such recorded cases, we shall cite only one which we are recording verbatim from the writings of Catherine Lassagne:

"One day a possessed woman came to the confessional of *Monsieur le Curé* to confess her sins. She suffered from attacks of possession only from time to time, and was perfectly calm at all other times. When her turn came, *Monsieur le Curé* kept urging her to begin. Then the following dialogue took place:

"The Devil, speaking through the lips of the possessed woman said aloud, because those around the confessional heard the entire conversation:

"'I have committed only one sin, and I offer this beautiful fruit to all who want to share it. Raise your hand: absolve me. You sometimes raise it for me. I am often with you in the confessional.

"*Monsieur le Curé*, in Latin: *'Tu, quis es?'* [Who are you?]

"The Devil: *'Magister caput!'* [The commander-in-chief!]

"'Black toad, you make me suffer so much! You are always saying you want to go away!... Why don't you go? Why don't you go to the big banquets?...'

"*Monsieur le Curé*: 'I don't have time.'

"The Devil: 'Others take time, don't they? Why do you preach such simple sermons? Everyone thinks you are an ignoramus!...'

"'The purple robe (the Bishop of Belley) has written you.... I made him forget one of the things he wanted to tell you....'

"*Monsieur le Curé* said later he had received a letter from his bishop, but no one else could know about it because he had told no one.

"*Monsieur le Curé*: 'I shall write to His Excellency asking him to authorize me to drive you out of the body of this woman.'

"The Devil: 'I shall make your hand tremble so hard that you won't be able to write. Black toad! I'll get you! I have beaten stronger men than you!... You're not dead yet?... If it were not for the B... who is up there (referring to the Blessed Virgin with a vulgar word)—we'd have gotten you! But she protects you too much, and that big dragon at the door of the church...(the chapel of St. Michael and the Holy Angels, at the entrance of the church).'"

The dialogue went on. The Devil uttered insults against Bishop Devie of Belley; against Bishop de Bonald of Puy, soon to be named Archbishop of Lyons; against certain priests, and finally against the Curé of Ars himself. But he could find only praiseworthy actions to condemn:

"Tell me, why do you get up so early in the morning? You are disobeying the purple robe!"

The account does not say who had the last word, but very probably the Curé of Ars was the victor, as on other occasions.

Gradually the "infestations" of Satan became less frequent, especially after 1855. They ceased entirely about a year before the saint's death.

To quote the words of Abbé Trochu:

"The Devil did not come back any more, and Father Vianney had no regrets at the loss of such a comrade. He did not disturb him during his last agony, as has happened in the case of other saints. Even before the end of his earthly trials, the Curé of Ars had inflicted a definitive defeat upon Satan."

His Greatest Joy

Now that we have spoken of John Mary Vianney's trials and combats, it is time to talk of his joys and triumphs.

Beyond a doubt Father Vianney felt his greatest triumphs were the processions held at Ars in honor of the Feast of Corpus Christi. No effort was spared to make the occasion magnificent, and the canopy given by Viscount Prosper des Garets enhanced it appreciably. As we have already mentioned, it was in 1826 that the entrance to the church was widened to permit the passage of the canopy.

A brochure printed in 1852 and entitled *Album: Le Pèlerinage d'Ars* (Album: The Pilgrimage of Ars), by an anonymous author who signed himself Ad. C., cites that these celebrations were at the origin of what came to be called the "pilgrimage of Ars." And this pilgrimage was indeed one of the more extraordinary religious phenomena of 19th-century France, together with the apparitions of the Blessed Virgin Mary at Lourdes and La Salette.

According to this profusely illustrated brochure: "The peregrinations to Ars began over twenty-five years ago. At the time of the Feast of Corpus Christi the faithful of the surrounding villages and towns would go there to view the annual exhibition of richly adorned vestments and sacred objects given through the piety and generosity of the former lords of Ars. These gifts are said to be very valuable, especially a canopy, a monstrance, and several magnificent banners....

"During the splendid processions for Corpus Christi there is a majestic exodus from the village church, priests in copes of cloth of gold surrounding the monstrance adorned with many rubies, and there is a vast crowd in attendance. In former days, we repeat, all these treasures were exhibited for the

The Curé himself would go to Lyons to select liturgical objects and vestments for his church. This chasuble shows that he spared no expense when it came to the liturgy.

faithful to admire for a week's time, and that was how the fame of the church of Ars began. Nowadays, there are still many visitors constantly coming and going, but this is because of the reputation for holiness of *Monsieur le Curé* Vianney...."

The important fact to remember is that the pilgrimage of Ars, of which we shall have much to say, originated in the Eucharistic triumph secured through the devotion of our holy pastor.

It is no exaggeration to say that the Feast of Corpus Christi was the supreme moment of joy in the entire year both for Father Vianney and his parishioners.

The Feast of Corpus Christi at Ars

In the *Album* mentioned above, the anonymous author writing in 1847 refers to his own eyewitness experiences. His style is somewhat romantic, giving it old-fashioned charm and local color.

As he relates it, it was entirely by chance that he came to visit Ars:

"Sitting down to rest on a hillock at the edge of the prairies that stretched out before me like a green ocean, I held my head in my hands and fell into a deep reverie.

"All of a sudden the sound of festive artillery echoed loudly to the north of the valley. A triple salute came from the south in response. At this signal the village bell started to peal furiously. Looking toward Ars, I could see a large crowd around the church which was too small to hold so many people. On roads leading to the church I could discern horses proceeding swiftly toward the celebration. I also seemed to see flags flying from the turrets of the neighboring château, and others flying from the belfry of the village church.

"Finally I understood it was the Feast of Corpus Christi, celebrated throughout our countryside for the past twenty years. I went down into the valley, toward the sound of the voices singing hymns in unison. What pomp greeted my surprised eyes! A vast procession made up of pilgrims from every region advanced under different banners, heading out into the fields. Among them were the poor women of *La Providence*, dressed in rough serge, then came some nuns whose accent and vivacious, sunburned faces revealed them to be from southern France.

"Still further on, came rich and elegant women, then young men of obvious means, as well as others, whose halting gait bespoke a life of hard labor or of debauchery.

"Every minute, the local artillery rang out solemnly, and was answered by a detonation from the château to the south.

"The procession advanced. The canopy of gold cloth, the gilded monstrance, the brocaded capes, shown in the sun's rays filtering through the large trees. The old man, the revered pastor of the village walked slowly, carrying the God of all!

"Meanwhile, on the border between the village and the property of the château a beautiful repository had been set up. The incense smoked in the censers, rising into the rays of the setting sun amid the dark green leaves of the trees. The procession advanced, singing hymns as it passed under the elegant arches. Soon the canopy stopped. Two thousand persons knelt, bowed their heads toward the warm earth, as the priest with trembling hands slowly raised the monstrance and blessed everyone in the name of the Father!..."

Then the procession moved on. At the château, a second repository had been set up. Again, a volley of artillery fire, again the incensing with the censers.

Again, the blessing with the Blessed Sacrament to the sound of a silvery bell.

Finally the procession returned to the village church the same way it had come.

For Father Vianney, these were days of deepest joy and fulfillment. We can easily understand that after seeing the holy priest's face transfigured with happiness during these ceremonies, everyone felt drawn to him. He seemed to them like another Jesus Christ. That is why so many came to him with the kind of trust that Christ had once inspired in the crowds of Galilee.

It was indeed the Feast of Corpus Christi at Ars, with its canopy and brocades, its banners and hymns, that explains the origin and growth of the pilgrimage of Ars we are about to describe.

The Pilgrimage of Ars

To See a Saint

The pilgrimage of Ars began around 1827 and kept growing larger every year until the saint's death in 1859. Since his death, it has continued under a new form until the present time. Nothing like it had been seen since the days of the Gospel and of the baptism of John the Baptizer in the Jordan, or more recently since the days of St. Vincent Ferrer. Jesus could have asked the pilgrims of Ars the same question he asked the Jews of his own time: "What did you go out to the wasteland to see?" (Mt. 11:7)

"A reed swaying in the wind?" No, then what? A man in sumptuous garments? Certainly not! The *Album*, cited earlier, describes our saint in these words:

"Father Vianney is a man...of medium height, with a slender body, an excessively thin and pale face, exhausted by sickness and fasting: hollow cheeks, prominent cheekbones, a penetrating gaze reminiscent of the expressions of the Spanish saints, eyes filled with an indefinable expression portrayed by Zurbaran or Murillo...."

So this is what people came to see! A poor country pastor. The pastor of one of the smallest and most insignificant parishes in all of France.

What was at the bottom of this mystery?

At first, people came to admire the splendor of the celebration of the Feast of Corpus Christi and its Octave, the magnificence of the canopy and the banners deployed for the occasion. Afterward, people would come back to see the pastor, to consult him, to confide their troubles and sins to him, and to receive God's absolution from his hand.

Evidently, it was possible to receive absolution in any Catholic parish. The difference was that here the words were spoken by a saint.

A saint! These words explain everything. Otherwise this whole story is incomprehensible.

As soon as Father Vianney was appointed to the parish of Ars, his friends from Dardilly, Ecully, and Les Noës began to visit him. And yet they cannot be considered as the originators of the "pilgrimage."

During the Jubilee of 1826 the Curé of Ars had preached at the celebrations of all the neighboring parishes. Many people had thus come to know him, and they continued to seek him out. Even so, the pilgrimage was to become something far more impressive. People would come to Ars not only from the surrounding area but from all of France.

The Impetus

The impetus to the pilgrimage was given by a few simple and devout persons who had not thought of starting an organized movement. Here again we obtain valuable information from the *Album* of 1852, in the words of an eyewitness who viewed events in the light of the time:

"See these men on the road to Ars. They keep walking, impelled by an inner voice, leaning on a staff and sometimes trudging on in their bare feet. They keep going in the dust, in sunshine and in rain, suffering hunger and thirst—which for them is a sweet sacrifice—and they hasten toward the pilgrimage of Ars as if they hoped to find everything the poor and afflicted can ever need. There they expect to find words straight from the soul to soften the bitterness of tears, consolation and brotherly love to dispel life's sorrows.

"Let us watch them as they go by. Here are some peasants, who confront the inclemencies of the weather, till the soil, and plant some of their own strength into the soil as they sow their crops. Where are they from? From the cloud-covered land of Dombes, with its misty landscape....

"When you watch these pallid faces, these men shivering with fever like the last leaves on the birch trees in an autumn wind, when you see them going to seek consolation at Ars, do not accuse them of heedlessness, rather, pity them.

"Look once more at these strangers. They come in great numbers from Forez, Rive-de-Gier, Saint-Etienne. They live out their lives deep in the earth, and grow old at the hard labor [of mining]. Some of them have whispered to each other today: 'We suffer too much in body and soul.... We must set out for the distant village of Ars where there is a priest who prays and weeps with the unfortunate.'

"Still others—and they are many—come from Lyons, the city of two rivers, where there is a whir of activity day and night. They are silk-weavers, producing many different fabrics. Usually they are short, jaundiced-looking, thin, slightly hump-backed.

They are victims of industry, that unbelievable lever of progress and suffering in modern times...."

Following these throngs of poor people come the wealthy, those who are bored with life, the curious, the thoughtful, the worried, those who are searching, who need God, who need peace, forgiveness, faith and love.

A Swelling Creek

This movement began in a very small way, like a creek flowing out of a spring, but it never dried up. It kept growing until it was a great river.

As early as 1827, according to John Pertinand, the teacher who was a great friend of the Curé of Ars, about twenty pilgrims came to Ars daily. That added up to about seven or eight thousand a year. The *Album* cited above states that by 1852 there were about 20,000 visitors to Ars each year. During the last years of Father Vianney's life, a local carter who was particularly well-informed estimated that 80,000 persons came in public conveyances and that the total number of pilgrims was between 100,000 and 120,000 annually. By the year 1858-1859, the creek had grown into a mighty river.

Catherine Lassagne commented on it to her pastor:

"*Monsieur le Curé*, other missionaries run after sinners, even into foreign lands, but it seems that sinners run after you."

And he answered with a smile:

"That's not far from the truth!"

Opposition

Let no one imagine that the continuous flow of people toward Ars aroused no opposition. At the start the clergy showed no enthusiasm for this expression of religious fervor and holy curiosity. On the contrary, they were in the forefront of those who tried to stop it.

This is not surprising. Humanly speaking, nothing can be more vexing to a shepherd of souls than to note that on the eve of every feastday the best of his flock desert the parish to go and worship somewhere else! And where were they going? To an unknown village whose pastor had very little education and knew no theology, who had been admitted to Holy Orders purely as a favor, a pastor who was shabbily dressed and scarcely presentable, whose teaching was of questionable worth, and in any case very commonplace. And to think they could find a thousand times better guidance in their own parish!

After all, wasn't this fad, this craze scandalous, dangerous, and utterly absurd?

Various pastors tried to deter their flocks from taking part in the pilgrimage to Ars. They even spoke against it from the pulpit. To make their point more convincingly, some of them attributed to the Curé of Ars all sorts of statements he had never made but that were being bandied about by misinformed or fanatical pilgrims.

Commenting on it all, Father Vianney said:

"Poor little Curé of Ars! People claim he has said and done so many things!... Now the sermons are about him and not about the Gospel!..."

He received letters, for the most part anonymous, insulting and condemning him, and even threatening to denounce him to his bishop. And soon such threats were in fact carried out. Here is a sample of these letters by the young pastor of a neighboring parish:

"*Monsieur le Curé*, anyone who knows as little theology as you should not enter a confessional!..."

And here is Father Vianney's answer, which can be regarded as exemplifying his attitude:

"My very dear and very revered confrere, I have so many reasons to love you! You are the only person who has really known me well. Since you are so kind and charitable as to take an interest in my poor soul, please help me to obtain the favor I have been asking for so long, that I may be replaced in a post of which I am unworthy because of my ignorance, so I can retire into some little corner to weep over my poor life. I have so much penance to do! I have so much atonement to make! And so many tears to shed!"

By dint of humility, gentleness, patience, and also by reason of the proofs he gave of his supernatural gifts, he finally disarmed all his opponents and in the end won the support of the clergy. That is why a time came when the most distinguished churchmen of France—Lacordaire, Combalot, bishops, prelates—joined the ranks of the pilgrims to Ars. Bishop de Langalerie insisted on going to confession to him as an ordinary penitent among all the others. In later years he said that after the Curé had heard his confession, he simply gave him this advice:

"Your Excellency, love your priests very much!"

A Saint's Day

The pilgrimage, the continuous influx of people knocking on his rectory door and coming to his church had made a profound change in his way of life. This triumph became his most excruciating cross. He became the slave of sinners. His whole life now consisted in hearing confessions, preaching, praying, and fasting.

There was an unbelievable monotony to his life. Catherine Lassagne has described one of his typical days in her memoirs, *Cahier des Souvenirs*, which will give us a pretty accurate idea of what his life was to be like from that time on:

"Here's how he spent his day: Rising some-times at midnight and other times at two, but most often at one o'clock in the morning, he would go to the church with his lighted candle. A large crowd of people who had spent the night in the belfry were waiting for him. Certain devoted men had to keep guard every night to maintain a little order in the church, because everybody pushed the door open at once wanting to go to confession right away, which was impossible. Some would beg the others to let them go first, but those who had been waiting their turn — sometimes for several days — were in no mood to yield their place.

"It was often observed that he would single out certain persons from the crowd and beckon to them to come to his confessional. The others didn't dare complain because they felt God had revealed to him the reasons that impelled these individuals to speak to him without delay.

"He would arrive at the church and pass be-tween two rows of pilgrims. Not only did these fill the chapel of St. John where he had his confessional, but they often stretched out to the altar of the chapel of the Blessed Virgin. In addition to these lines of penitents there were many others throughout the church who wanted to go to confession.

"When he reached the chapel he would kneel on the altar step and pray for a few minutes. Very often he would recite several *Our Fathers* with his penitents before entering the confessional, to ask God to give them the proper dispositions. He would advise them to say the *Confiteor* before coming to him, in order to give himself a little time.

"He would enter the confessional and usually remain there up to seven hours. Then he came out to say Mass. After Mass he would bless various holy objects in the sacristy, make enrollments in confraternities, write his name on pictures, especially pictures of the Blessed Virgin, upon which various individuals or families had written out their consecration to Mary Immaculate.

"Then he would go home to eat a frugal meal, and return to the church. He would hear the men's confessions in the sacristy until eleven o'clock. Here too, volunteer guards maintained order, for there were often a large number of men, as well as women, waiting to go to confession. When he wanted to recite his Office, he would ask whoever was in the confessional in the sacristy to remain until he was finished, so he could pray in peace.

"At eleven o'clock he taught his catechism class, which lasted forty-five minutes, or an hour at most. After the catechism class, he would often go and hear the confessions of persons who were in a hurry and to whom he had given appointments. These individuals would be waiting for him at another confessional, because his own was always surrounded by a crowd of penitents.

"When he was ready to leave the church he usually had some difficulty because there were always others who still wanted to go to confession. But a Brother or some other guard would open a way through the crowd so he could go out.

"Once back in his rectory, he ate his light meal. He didn't lose much time at it. Sometimes he allowed himself barely five minutes for his dinner. He ate so little! Then he would rest for a few moments. During this short interval, there were people waiting for him at all the rectory doors. Everybody asked the others by what door he would pass because they wanted to see him and talk with him. He often slipped out through the door to the garden. The minute they caught sight of him, everyone would run full speed to meet him. There was such a crowd that he could not satisfy everybody. They would surround him, several people speaking to him at once. Some would take hold of his arm, others would pull him. There was great confusion. If there had not been one or more devoted men to protect him—Messrs. Oriol, de La Bastie, Claude Virer, or Brother Jerome—I think the crowd would have made him fall, and perhaps trampled on him! His guards would accompany him to visit the Missionaries. There, too, people were waiting to talk to him and ask his advice.

"After a short visit with these gentlemen who were happy to see him for a few moments, he returned to the church. The Missionaries accompanied him to protect him from the crush of pilgrims. And so he arrived at the church, where a large number of people wanted to go to confession. As he approached, the news spread among the people and they rushed to meet him. Many asked to be taken out of turn. He would grant this favor to a few whose needs he knew. Remembering he was a pastor, he tended to give preference to members of the parish.

"He would kneel for an instant on the altar step of St. John, and then he was back in the confessional. This was usually around one o'clock in the afternoon. He stayed there until four. He would come out for a few minutes and then go to the sacristy to hear the confessions of the men. If there happened to be a few women who had serious reasons for not waiting their turn, he would hear them in another confessional, before the men. For several years he had been hearing confessions until seven o'clock in the evening during the winter, and later in the summer.

"When he came out of the confessional he would go to the pulpit and recite the rosary and other prayers with all who were present. Then he would return to his rectory, always escorted by his guards. A way was opened for him through the crowd, from the door of the belfry to the door of his courtyard.

As he came into view, everyone on his path would kneel. He would give a general blessing before going in, and the door closed behind him. Once he was inside, Brother Jerome followed him to his room, to perform whatever services he could for him, such as lighting his fire, etc., and returned to the church.

"His hours of rest were very short, and we don't know how many hours of the night he spent resting. How much time did he devote to prayer, macerations, and reading? God was the only witness. It is known, however, that during the last years of his life he spent many nights in physical pain. A fever of some sort robbed him almost completely of rest. But when his accustomed time to get up arrived, he did not renege. He walked with difficulty. As he went about his duties as a confessor, he often seemed about to fall. Even so, he said he felt more comfortable when he was up than lying down. He continued this mode of life until his last illness...."

What can we add to such an account? It would be hard to give a more vivid description of a man besieged and hounded by his relentless admirers. He was, as Father Chevrier has said, a "man consumed" by his vocation.

Another Description

If we want another witness to his way of life, we can turn again to the *Album du Pèlerinage*. Its anonymous author agrees substantially with Catherine Lassagne.

"*Monsieur le Curé* spends the greater part of his time in his church. Ordinarily he leaves it at ten or eleven o'clock at night—during the summer, of course—and returns about four o'clock in the morning. He eats only one meal a day, and he makes sure his food consists of the most common vegetables.

"The rectory where he lives is next to the church; his bedroom is on the second floor. The walls of this room are bare. An old chest, a few pictures of saints, some old theology books, these make up the entire furnishings. He sleeps on a mat with a straw bolster. He never makes a fire, even in winter." Actually, toward the end of his life, he did make a fire of twigs in his fireplace during the winter.

In trying to evaluate our saint's personality, the *Album* continues in its rather stilted style:

"He is not a somber and melancholy man whose senses are in a state of languor and inaction, and whose mind is confused by anger, continuous meditation, ascetic ecstasies and pseudo-prophetic revelations.

"Even less is this worthy priest under the spell of catalepsy, a sad and rare symptom of fanaticism, indeed an illness in which the soul seems withdrawn into the head and absent from the whole body, which for its part is subject at times to heavenly convulsions.

"No, no. Neither melancholy nor visions, none of those symptoms are to be found in the man we have observed at first hand and of whom we speak. On the contrary, a consuming activity allows him almost no time for the rest indispensable for life.

"His mind and heart, it is true, have made an irrevocable choice. But this choice, this idea, this sentiment is translated in him by the words: God and love of neighbor!

"His heart has never been touched nor his mind tormented by arrogant knowledge, riches, and human honors for which the crowd strives, laments, and constantly aspires. He deals with such things only to make his penitents understand their cruel emptiness and transitory nature. God who rewards and sustains love of neighbor, who relieves and consoles—this is all the good priest knows, and especially all that he teaches with admirable efficacy...."

These passages confirm the publicly attested fact that over a period of more than thirty years the holy Curé of Ars heard confessions on an average of fifteen to sixteen hours a day, with short intervals not for rest but for prayer, for reciting his breviary, or for his daily catechism classes. He carried his cross unremittingly during those thirty years, with a few interruptions due to illness. In 1843, everyone thought he was dying, but he is said to have been cured by the intervention of the Blessed Virgin Mary and of his "dear little Philomena." His labors were also temporarily interrupted when on two or three occasions he was driven to abandon his work and his parish.

We can readily estimate that hundreds of thousands of penitents passed through his various confessionals, either in the chapel of St. John the Baptizer where the women came, or in the sacristy where he heard the men's confessions. What was the nature of his influence on souls, and how can we evaluate and explain this influence? We shall try to answer this question in our next chapter.

The Gift
of Prophecy-
Spiritual Favors

The Gift of Prophecy

All biographies of St. John Mary Vianney, and especially the one by Abbé Trochu which is the best,[1] are filled with extraordinary facts relating to what some might call his "gift of intuition." The saint's reputation was built on these facts which explain in great part the weight attributed by so many to even his most trivial statements. The *Annales d'Ars* have published some of them in recent times that were not yet widely known.

We shall group these happenings under the title "The Gift of Prophecy." As we see it, this title conforms more closely to Christian tradition and history than the term "gift of intuition." The word "prophecy" also has the advantage of suggesting a supernatural gift.

---

1. Abbé Francis Trochu, *The Curé d'Ars, St. Jean-Marie Baptiste Vianney (1786-1859)*, translated by Dom Ernest Graf, O.S.B., Westminster, Md.: The Newman Press, 1960.

Throughout the early Church the gifts of the Holy Spirit or *charisms* were distributed in great abundance, as St. Paul has repeatedly indicated. In enumerating these charismatic gifts, the Apostle gives special importance to the gift of prophecy, which he describes in this way: "The prophet... speaks to men for their upbuilding, their encouragement, their consolation" (1 Cor. 14:3).

This is precisely what the Curé of Ars did in an outstanding way. However, when we attribute the gift of prophecy to him we want to go still further. We are thinking especially of his wonderful gift of reading into the consciences of others.

Specific examples of his gift of prophecy will be more convincing than any amount of speculation on our part.

A Few Facts

We do not claim the Curé of Ars knew the sins of his penitents even before they confessed them. Even so, it is certain that in many cases he anticipated their admissions, expressed their statements clearly, and completed their partial declarations so as to give the full story.

Example: An unbeliever came with some friends, but had no intention of confessing his sins. The Curé of Ars happened to pass by in the church. He paused, began looking around him and beckoned to the man, much to the latter's surprise. Without hesitating, the man mechanically obeyed and came forward.

"It's a long time since you've been to confession," said Abbé Vianney, as he shook hands with him.

"My good Father," the man answered, "it's something like thirty years, I think."

"Thirty years, my friend?... Think again. Thirty-three years ago, you were in such a place!..."

"You're right, *Monsieur le Curé.*"

"Then, we are ready for confession now, aren't we?"

The old man was completely overcome, shamed, and transformed. He obeyed, and his confession lasted twenty minutes.

"I immediately experienced an indefinable sense of well-being," he later reported.

Another incident has been related by a fine Christian lady, Mademoiselle Cognon, who died in 1947 at Châtillon-sur-Chalaronne. It concerns her own grandmother, from whom she had heard it many times.

It seems that Mlle. Cognon's grandmother had come all the way from Auvergne to receive absolution from the Curé of Ars. She was afflicted with an illness, and had consulted one of those healers known as "sorcerers" in the French countryside. The healer had given her a bottle containing some sort of remedy.

As the good lady approached Ars on foot, she decided to hide the sorcerer's phial in a thicket. She then proceeded to the village church, where she went to confession with great devotion. What was her surprise to hear the holy confessor say:

"My good child, you aren't telling me about that phial you hid in the bushes!"

The amazed lady hastened to confess her "crime," and wept profusely as she received absolution.

Around the year 1840, a certain *"Père Rochette"* brought his crippled child to Ars. His wife came with him. While she went to confession and received Communion, the father was totally concerned with obtaining a miraculous cure for his son. He didn't even respond to the Curé of Ars' invitation to enter the confessional. Turning to the man's wife, the priest said:

"So he's that much of an unbeliever!" Then he once again invited him to approach the confessional. This time *Père Rochette* came forward.

"It's between the two of us, now, *Père Rochette*," said the Curé. "Enter!" And he pointed to the confessional.

"I really don't feel like it," was the answer.
"Begin," the priest answered simply.
Père Rochette fell on his knees and stammered:
"Father, it's been quite a while since.... Ten years...."

"Or perhaps a little more...."
"Twelve years...."
"Still a little more...."
"Yes," answered Rochette, "since the great Jubilee of 1826."
"Now we've got it! If we try hard enough, we can remember!"

And so *Père Rochette* finished his confession, weeping as he spoke. He received Communion. When the Rochettes left Ars, their son was walking without crutches.

There have been hundreds of such incidents reported, not by the confessor who was bound by the inviolable secrecy of the confessional, but by the happy benefactors of his "intuitions." We would call them simply "acts of prophecy."

We could fill volumes with accounts of like nature. And in fact many such volumes have been published.

The Curé of Ars could read men's hearts — and women's too, of course. He often saw into the future as well. He would counsel one young woman to get married, and another to enter the convent, even indicating the religious congregation where she would find peace of soul.

When a sinner confessed his sins almost mechanically and cynically, without the slightest contrition, he would respond by bursting into tears himself.

"Why are you crying so much, Father?" one of these unrepentant sinners asked.

"My friend, I weep because you do not weep enough!"

From his side of the confessional, he sometimes uttered groans and sighs that would soften the hardest heart. Rarely did anyone leave his tribunal of penance without being overcome with contrition for his or her sins.

His knowledge of the most hidden concerns of those who came to him went far beyond the limits of natural extrasensory perception, as we now call it.

The *Annales d'Ars* for the year 1912-1913 reported the following case. A lady from the area of Montpellier had just inherited a large fortune. However she had long been thinking of entering the religious life. Her problem was: what should she do with her inheritance? Her spiritual director, Father Pacalin, a Jesuit, had not given her any decisive answer on the matter. When she thought of going to consult the Curé of Ars, Father Pacalin approved. Once at the pilgrimage site she mingled with the crowd, praying with all her heart.

At two o'clock the next morning, our saint arrived as usual to hear confessions. He knelt for his short prayer, and turning around he went straight to the lady whom he did not know and who was waiting in the chapel of St. Philomena.

"You are in a hurry, Mademoiselle," he said. "Come, I shall let you go first."

The young woman arose and followed Father Vianney. But she had scarcely begun to explain her problem to him, when he stopped her short:

"That's enough, my child, I know your problem."

He then went into details about what she should do with her fortune, and the charitable works she should support. Then he concluded with these strange words:

"Hurry, now! You have no time to lose!"

The young lady returned home, and asked her spiritual director how he had been able to reach the Curé of Ars so fast and tell him about her dilemma.

Father Pacalin was surprised. He said he had not written to Ars, and besides he considered himself under obligation to preserve secrecy. In any event, he would not have had the time to give the Curé of Ars the information in question.

The Curé had also told her to hurry. And so she made all the necessary arrangements at Montpellier and returned to Avignon to enter a convent. Very soon after arriving in this city, as she was coming out from a Mass at which she had received Communion, she became violently ill and died of cholera that very day.

Here we see clearly the foretelling of the unforeseeable. It is a perfect example of the gift of prophecy.

Another incident of similar nature occurred in 1857 or 1858. A lady who lived in the Ardèche region had some very difficult problems to solve in her personal life. She had asked advice of her son who was a priest well qualified to give her wise and prudent counsel. Even so, she had not followed his advice, but decided to consult the Curé whose reputation was known throughout France.

As she mingled with the pilgrims in the church of Ars, Father Vianney made his way through the crowd and stood in front of her. In a very confident tone, he asked her:

"What have you come here for? You had no need to come so far. Why don't you put your trust in what your son has told you? He gave you the right answer. You must go back home and do what he told you to do."

We can imagine the lady's surprise and humiliation in seeing her innermost thoughts revealed so accurately before she had said a word, especially as the Curé of Ars did not know her personally. This incident was told by the lady's son, some twenty years after the death of Father Vianney.

These few examples should suffice. They do not really add much to what we already know about our saint. But they clearly point to the superior insights given to him from above for the guidance of souls.

The Wellspring

Without intentionally referring to himself, he once said:

"Those who are led by the Holy Spirit think right thoughts. That is why there are so many unlettered people who know more than the scholars!"

On one occasion there was discussion of John Mary Vianney in the presence of an eminent professor of philosophy. Someone said:

"There is holiness in the Curé of Ars, but that's all there is...."

The professor responded:

"On the contrary he is a man filled with great insights. They leap out of his conversations on all kinds of subjects. When we see things in the light of the Holy Spirit, we see so very clearly, we see so much beauty! For He raises us up to great heights of sensitivity and thought!"

Catherine Lassagne expressed the same sentiment:

"*Monsieur le Curé* was so small, so insignificant in his own eyes that the Holy Spirit was pleased to fill this void with Himself, giving him an abundance of admirable insights."

This presence of the Holy Spirit is precisely what we are talking about when we said Father John Mary Vianney possessed the gift of prophecy.

We must remember that charisms, as they are called, are freely given by God, that they do not constitute sanctity. While they can be an outward sign of holiness, their purpose is not so much to benefit those who receive them as to enlighten and sanctify others through their charismatic gifts. Thus, St. Joan of Arc's "Voices" were given her so that France might be saved but added nothing to her personal holiness.

When we discuss the spirituality and holiness of the Curé of Ars in the next chapter, we shall make no reference to this gift of prophecy which, as we have tried to show, he possessed in abundance. For this gift had no direct relationship to his intrinsic sanctity.

Miracles?

The same holds true of the miracles attributed to him during his lifetime. We report some of them here only to be faithful to our documentary sources. These miracles were also gifts freely bestowed by God, charisms, signs of holiness but not constituent elements of his holiness.

There was never any call to study these miracles in a canonical way. In this respect they were entirely different from the miracles obtained after his death through his intercession. As we know, the Church requires incontestable proof of several miracles through the intercession of a candidate for canonization. These miracles, which must have been obtained after the death of the servant of God in question, are subjected to very stringent examination. It is on the conclusions of these examinations that the Church passes canonical judgment.

We are under no obligation, therefore, to accept the miracles the Curé of Ars performed during his lifetime, except as historically authenticated facts attested to by sincere, competent and irrefutable witnesses.

The Multiplication of the Flour

Let us cite Catherine Lassagne's account of this miracle. While she was not the only witness to it, she did make a firsthand report on it.

"Once when we were at *La Providence*, we did not have enough flour to bake an ovenful of bread. Was the mill out of order? I don't know. In any event, it could not grind the wheat we had sent over to be ground. At most, all that was left in the house was enough flour to bake three loaves of bread, because it seems a bit exaggerated to claim we could have baked four. Anyway, we took this small amount of flour and kneaded it, and the kneading trough was as full of dough as on the days when we put a large sack of flour into it. We baked ten large loaves, each weighing 20 to 22 pounds, and we filled the oven as usual to the great astonishment of those of us who witnessed it.

"One of us said to our co-worker who usually kneaded the dough — Jeanne Marie Chanay: 'We shall be without bread, since we can't get any flour....' 'Why don't we cook the rest of the flour,' she answered. 'It's very little, but it would be something.' 'I thought about that, but I want to ask *Monsieur le Curé's* advice.'

"And *Monsieur le Curé* thought it best to cook whatever flour was left. Did he petition God for this multiplication, or did he simply ask God to take care of his children? I have no idea. Of this, however, there can be no doubt. We are convinced this miracle was worked because of the holy Curé."

Multiplication of the Pumpkin Squash

Still speaking of her beloved master, Catherine Lassagne continued:

"He enjoyed coming from time to time to serve his children at mealtime. This did not happen often, however. One day, I had a platter of pumpkin squash in my hands and noticed there was not enough to go around. I was dismayed. *Monsieur le Curé* arrived as I was about to serve his children, took the platter out of my hands and served them in abundance, giving a large portion to each one. I was worried as I saw the large portions he was serving, and so I went up to him and whispered: 'But *Monsieur le Curé*, there won't be enough for those at the end of the table.'

"He made no answer and continued as before. I don't remember if there was any left over, but all the children were copiously served."

The Multiplication of the Wine

Catherine Lassagne's account continues:

"Another time, a full cask of wine had been completely spilt. *Monsieur le Curé* noticed what had happened, and said: 'You'd better go down to the cellar and take a look. I think your wine is disappearing.'

"We went down at once and found the cask absolutely empty. We began as best we could to collect whatever was left of the clearest wine from the sand. We managed to salvage two little pails of wine, which we poured into another cask that was almost empty, I believe. We kept drawing from that cask for several more days, until there was probably almost none left.

"Next to this cask, there was a *cempotte*—a barrel holding 100 liters—from which 50 liters of wine had already been drawn. So there were only fifty left. The contents of the *cempotte* were poured into the large empty cask, with a capacity of 200 bottles. To the great astonishment of Jeanne Marie Chanay and Marie Filliat who were attending to this matter, the *cempotte's* contents filled the cask. Jeanne Marie began to laugh, and said teasingly: 'See if the cask is full!'

"'Yes,' Marie answered, 'look. I can touch wine with my finger.' Then both of them were convinced it was a miracle.

"That day I noticed *Monsieur le Curé* did not seem disturbed when he came to warn us that the wine had been spilt. He said it was just an accident that the good God could easily rectify."

The Miracle of the Wheat

Marie Filliat, the newest of the three directors of *La Providence*, was inclined to believe it was a miracle because upon her arrival in 1830 her colleagues had told her about an extraordinary happening of the same nature that had occurred in the rectory's attic.

We can therefore situate the following incident sometime around 1829.

The Curé of Ars always kept a supply of wheat in the rectory attic. But one day he discovered there were only a few handfuls left on the floor. This was a serious blow to him, for the crop had not been good that year and he could not ask the parish for wheat. Of course there was Mlle. d'Ars, the very generous lady of the manor, but she had been called upon so many times before! Sadly, the Curé decided he would have to send home some of the orphan girls since he didn't have enough to feed them.

For a man of his burning charity, this was a painful sacrifice. He decided to seek God's help through the intercession of St. Francis Regis. As we have already noted, he had once made a pilgrimage to this saint's shrine at La Louvesc. He fully realized he was now asking for a genuine miracle. But this was to be first of all an "evangelical" miracle, and Jesus had promised so much to those who had *faith*!

Going to the attic, Father Vianney swept all the scattered grains of wheat into a single pile. Then he hid a little relic of St. Francis Regis inside the tiny mound. Besides, he called upon his little schoolgirls to pray fervently with him that God would provide their "daily bread."

Then he quietly waited for heaven's answer to his request.

When Jeanne Marie Chanay, who was the baker at *La Providence*, came to tell him the wheat bin was empty, he answered simply and with apparent unconcern:

"Why don't you go and get the wheat that is left in the attic...."

She obeyed, thinking to herself that there must not be much of anything left up there. What was her surprise, as she tried to push the door open, to feel a weight pressing against it. The door would hardly open at all, and through the crack wheat began to pour out.

She rushed downstairs and shouted to *Monsieur le Curé*:

"So you wanted to test my obedience! The attic is full!"

"You say it's full?"

"Yes, it's running over. Come and see for yourself!"

They both went back up to the attic. They found it completely filled with wheat, and noticed that it was not of the same color as the old. There had never been so much wheat at one time at the rectory. Everyone was even surprised that the floor had not collapsed under the weight of it.

During the beatification process, Father Toccanier, who had been Father Vianney's curate toward the end of his life, related that the Curé had told him about it himself:

"I had many orphans to feed, and in the attic there was only a handful of wheat left. I figured that St. Francis Regis, who had miraculously fed the poor during his lifetime, would certainly do it again after his death. I had a relic of this saint. I placed it in with the little wheat that was left. The children prayed, and the attic was filled."

Note that in his account, the saint speaks as if he himself had done nothing. It was St. Francis Regis who did everything. It was the children who prayed. That is why he did not hesitate to talk about this miracle.

When Bishop Devie of Belley heard about this extraordinary happening, he decided to visit the attic where it had occurred. In an effort to get the Curé of Ars to talk, he asked him point-blank:

"You say the wheat reached up this high?" pointing to a spot high up on the wall.

"No, Your Excellency," answered the Curé, not realizing that he was being trapped, "higher than that, up to there!"

Through St. Philomena

One of the most reliable witnesses at the beatification process was John Pertinand, the local schoolteacher. He testified:

"However the servant of God knew that extraordinary things were happening in his parish. He even admitted a few times that much good was being done there, but he attributed everything to God or to the saints, especially St. Philomena."

The Curé of Ars made use of this unknown young martyr of the early Church to hide his own gifts as a miracle-worker, just as he had attributed the miracle of the wheat to St. Francis Regis. In this way he strove to spread devotion to St. Philomena throughout France. Thanks to him, the name of the little "nameless" saint became popular among the people of France, and came to be used widely as a baptismal name for little girls.

Actually, the pilgrims to Ars were not completely taken in by this subterfuge. They felt that if St. Philomena answered the petitions addressed to her, it was only when they passed through the Curé. When someone would say this to him, he would protest vigorously:

"I do not work miracles. I am only a poor ignorant man who once tended sheep.... Turn to St. Philomena. I have never asked for anything through her without receiving it."

He also said that his only real concern was the salvation of souls. On one occasion he even declared:

"I have a good mind to tell St. Philomena not to work any more miracles for the body. She must first of all cure souls. This poor cadaver that is destined to rot doesn't count for very much!"

Another stratagem he used was to ask St. Philomena to postpone the cures asked of her so that they occurred outside the parish. "That way," he would say with a smile, "no one sees or knows!"

In the end, however, all his efforts to hide his miracles came to naught. Quite a few cures have been attributed to a word spoken by the saint.

For instance, one day he happened to pass by a crippled woman leaning on crutches. He had pity on her and said:

"Come now, walk!"

As the woman hesitated, Abbé Toccanier who was present repeated:

"Why don't you walk since you have been told to do so?"

The woman immediately threw down her crutches and walked. As a crowd quickly formed, Father Vianney hastened to tell the woman who had been miraculously cured:

"Take your crutches with you!"

The documents of the Process include at least thirty occurrences of this kind, and others were added into the record afterwards. The fact remains that the Curé of Ars attributed no importance to miracles effecting bodily cures except in the measure that they helped to transform souls.

The biographers of our saint are right when they claim that the greatest miracle of Ars consisted in the life of its holy pastor. From a human point of view, we cannot help wondering whether it was possible to live such a life of penance and apostolic labor, with almost no food or sleep. We need to inquire into this life and discover its underlying inspiration.

The Spirituality of the Curé of Ars

Schools of Spirituality

God alone is holy. There is no holiness except through Him. The term "spirituality" had been applied to the method by which one goes to God. There are many different ways, and hence many different schools of spirituality. Evidently, there are certain unchanging laws that apply in all schools. God is Love, and one can come to Him only through love. We can be like Him only if we love. Only if we love can we be holy. But love manifests itself in many ways. Each life is a poem different from all the others. Every saint has his own particular path to follow as he ascends the mountain of God.

That is why there are many schools of spirituality, such as the Benedictine, the Franciscan, the Dominican, the Carmelite, the Ignatian, the French Berullian school, and so on.

There is an unfortunate tendency to try at all costs to fit individual cases into fixed frameworks and categories. Even so, it may be helpful, in our effort to understand the sanctity of the Curé of Ars, to inquire into the wellsprings from which he drew his inspiration to holiness.

Whenever we search for the models he followed, the examples that inspired him, our quest leads us back to the Fathers of the Desert.

Even if we did not know that he was constantly reading and rereading the *Lives of the Saints* and the *Sayings of the Fathers,* his inhuman fasts can only be compared to those John Cassian and Palladius have recorded for us.

The Curé of Ars used to say in utmost seriousness: "Ignorance and gluttony are my two great faults." Such words might surprise us if we did not remember that the hermits of the Egyptian desert accused themselves of "gormandizing" when they had eaten one more olive or date than the small number they had set once and for all as their daily limit. The Fathers of the Desert were formidable and truly inimitable in their fasting. The Curé of Ars strove mightily to follow in their footsteps.

Throughout his life he put up a relentless struggle against sensuality in eating and drinking. He reduced to a minimum the amount of food without which he would not have had the strength to work. He bemoaned the fact that he could not fast more than he did. He used to say regretfully that he had been much happier during his youth because then he had been able to remain without food not only for the better part of the day, but even for the better part of the week.

In addition to fasting, our Curé also deprived himself cruelly of sleep. This practice of vigils had been an integral part of the spirituality of the Fathers of the Desert. Men like St. Anthony of the Desert, St. Macarius, and St. Pacomus courageously practiced vigils.

After St. Anthony had spent a night in contemplation, he was known to complain that the sunrise interrupted his intense prayer by reminding him of the passage of time.

Father John Mary Vianney habitually limited to a minimum the rest he allowed his body, for the same reason that he limited the quantity of food he consumed. In this matter, he would tolerate no faltering, no complacency in his penance. He liked to say:

"I have a good *cadaver*; with a little food and one or two hours of sleep, I can resume my work...."

As we have already seen, he usually arose at one o'clock in the morning and returned to his room only about ten or eleven o'clock at night. We have many reasons to think that even this short interval between ten o'clock at night and one in the morning was also spent in prayer, reciting the breviary, reading the *Lives of the Saints*, and scourging himself.

Likewise in imitation of the ways of the ancient hermits, he scorned comfort in his sleeping arrangements, seeking instead to do penance even during his period of rest. When he arrived at Ars he first chose to sleep on some twigs in a corner of his kitchen. Shortly thereafter, because of the excruciating neuralgia brought on by the humidity on the ground floor, he had gone to sleep in his attic where he slept on the floor, resting his head on a log. Even when he finally found himself obliged to sleep in his bedroom, he insisted on using a hard bed covered only with a little straw.

All these privations, macerations, and instruments of penance were inspired by the Fathers of the Desert.

Devotion to the Blessed Trinity

And yet the Curé of Ars would have been strangely unfaithful to the spirituality of the Desert Fathers if he had attached any importance to these external practices. He knew that the only reason for subjugating the flesh was to liberate the spirit. He had read in the *Lives* of his beloved saints that their great and overriding concern was to live constantly in God's presence, to think only of God, fleeing from the world and all created things in order to seek refuge in the Uncreated, the Eternal, that is to say, in the most Blessed Trinity.

Instead of losing his way in various secondary devotional practices, he went straight to the essential, to the one God in three Persons, who alone is worthy of adoration and love, and who is the wellspring of all goodness and perfection.

In this sense, we must say that the great impetus of his spiritual life was toward God-Trinity. As an indication of this inner orientation, he always kept a symbolic picture representing the Trinity at the first page of his breviary. According to Catherine Lassagne who knew him so well:

"The first virtue of *Monsieur le Curé* was his faith in the Blessed Trinity."

She quoted him as saying:

"What great happiness it is to pray! Puny creatures like us, speaking to God who is so great, so powerful! When we pray and come to church to pray, we delight the three Persons of the Blessed Trinity. If we would only think and realize what this means! How fortunate a Christian is to be able to converse with God! What lofty function!..."

This was the reason for his immense devotion to the Sign of the Cross, the most ancient Christian expression in honor of the Blessed Trinity. Catherine Lassagne has spoken of it:

"Even when the crowd was waiting impatiently for him, as well as before and after each meal, I always saw him stop and make the Sign of the Cross slowly and with deep recollection."

Thus, an act that many Catholics and perhaps even many priests make mechanically took on for him the significance and beauty of an act of faith and love for the three Persons of the Blessed Trinity.

Citations from the Sayings of the Church Fathers

When we say that the Curé of Ars found his inspiration in the Fathers of the Desert we are not merely speaking from conjecture. On many occasions he cited them verbatim. There is an ancient collection written in Greek about the year 500 A.D., called the *Apophtegmata Patrum* or *Sayings of the Fathers.* In it we find the following passage:

"A brother came to Abbot Macarius of Egypt and said to him: 'Father, speak to me so that I may know how to be saved.' And the old man answered: 'Go to the cemetery and utter curses against the dead.' And so the brother went, uttered insults and threw stones at them. When he returned to the old man he told him what he had done. The old man asked: 'Didn't they say anything to you?' 'Nothing,' said the brother. 'Then go back tomorrow and say words of praise to them.' So the brother went and called them all sorts of beautiful names: apostles, saints, just men!

"Returning once more to the old man, he said: 'I praised them....' 'And they still didn't say anything?' the old man asked. 'Nothing,' said the brother.

"Then the elder said: 'You know what insults you hurled against them, without a word of response from them, and what praises you bestowed on them, still without any answer. Well then! If you want to be saved, be like a dead man. Do not be concerned either with the insults or compliments of men, and in that way you can be saved'" (Migne, P.G. Vol. 65, col. 272).

Now, as we know there had once been many bitter critics of the Curé of Ars among the clergy, trying to discredit him. Several times the Curé's friends urged him to defend himself, to answer the unjust attacks against him. But he used the story of Abbot Macarius in an abbreviated form to make his point:

"One day a saint commanded one of his monks: 'Go to the cemetery and say insulting things to the dead.' The monk obeyed, and when he returned the saint commanded him: 'What did they answer?' 'Nothing.' 'Well then, return and praise them.' The monk obeyed once more and came back. 'Did they answer you this time?' 'Still nothing.' 'Well then,' answered the saint, 'whether people insult you or praise you, do the same as the dead.'"

Another time, referring to persons who were distracted in their prayers, Father Vianney said in one of his catechism classes:

"Flies do not settle on boiling water. They fall only into cold or tepid water."

This comparison was also taken from the *Sayings of the Fathers*.

"A brother asked Abbot Poemenius to advise him. And he answered: 'When your pot is on the fire, neither flies nor any reptile can touch it. But when it is cold, that is when they can attack it. The same is true of the monk. As long as he remains occupied with spiritual actions, the enemy can find no means of triumphing over him" (Migne, P.G., Vol. 65, col. 349).

If we reflect on this thought of Abbot Poemenius we will understand the nature of the spirituality the Curé of Ars absorbed from the Fathers of the Desert. The whole point is to "keep the pot on the fire," that is to say, to make use of austerities, penances, fasts, and scourgings, so as to light the flame of love in one's heart. That is all that really matters. That is how true spiritual growth is attained.

If we felt we absolutely had to place the spirituality of the Curé of Ars in the context of a particular school, we would say that it drew from wellsprings even earlier than the Benedictine School. For St. Benedict, the patriarch of the monastic life in the West, also borrowed everything from the Fathers of the Desert. However, he adapted their teachings so as to practice them within the limits of what is humanly possible and with a love of moderation, in short, with the general attitude characteristic of the ancient Romans.

This is truly the same spirituality as that of the Fathers, but mitigated, acclimated, adapted to the prevailing temperaments of the West.

The Curé of Ars, with his heroic zeal, returned to the holy excesses of the ancient hermits.

Impulses and Attempts to Flee

In a sense, it can be said that even Father Vianney's various attempts to flee from his parish and its crushing burdens were inspired by the spirituality of the Fathers of the Desert. Although there were only two very clear-cut and even dramatic episodes of this kind in his life, the impulse to flee was a kind of continual obsession with him.

His head was not turned by his successes as confessor, spiritual director, and admired miracle-worker, or by the thousands of pilgrims who flocked to him. In fact, his only thought was how he could leave his parish as soon as possible. He expressed this desire to each of the bishops under whose jurisdiction he worked. More than once, he answered his detractors by asking them to intervene with the ecclesiastical authorities so that he might be relieved of his heavy pastoral burden.

Let us not be confused by the word "burden." It was not the burden itself that he dreaded and wanted to evade. It was not the labor involved that frightened him.

On the contrary. In the footsteps of his ancient models, the most famous hermits and ascetics of the past, he yearned only for solitude, contemplation, and continual dialogue with his God, free from distractions and interruptions. What a joy that would have been for him! What penances, what macerations, fasts, he could have undertaken!

His deepest wish was to practice the spirituality of a hermit, and instead he was constantly besieged by unending tides of people. There is an astonishing contrast between his actual vocation and the great inner dream of his love for the Blessed Trinity. Sometimes he gently complained that he never obtained for himself the favors, or at least the principal favor he asked for: the privilege of withdrawing into the prayerful solitude of the heroes of silence and contemplation.

All who are called to exercise apostolic activity within the Church should learn from his example of the need to root action in contemplation. The underlying foundation of his never-ending apostolic activity was his interior union with God alone, in the silence of his soul.

The First Flight in 1843

The Curé of Ars' two flights or attempts to flee can readily be understood in the light of what we have just said about the roots of his spiritual life. They were in a sense part of his desire for union with God in the solitude of contemplation.

The first flight occurred in 1843. He was just recovering from an illness that his physician had expected to be fatal. He had been obliged to stop hearing the confessions of the pilgrims, and had taken quite a while to regain his health.

To help him carry out his functions, his bishop had sent Abbé Raymond, the pastor of Savigneux, the nearest parish to Ars. While this priest held the Curé of Ars in high esteem, he nurtured the secret ambition of replacing him. It almost seems as if he had been providentially sent to Father Vianney to exercise the latter's patience and humility.

According to Catherine Lassagne, "Father Raymond acted with the best of intentions in forcing Father Vianney to change the method and tempo of his priestly activities. The servant of God had all the more merit, for good was still being accomplished, in one way or another.... However, he had great love for his curate,...went along with his wishes whenever he could, and defended him on every occasion."

So the Curé of Ars' desire to slip away from his parish and leave it in the hands of another cannot be attributed to vexation or any purely human consideration.

In any case, he had often said that a pastor should never die in his own parish, but should retire long enough to do penance and prepare to appear before his sovereign Judge.

That is why in September, 1843, when he had recovered from the illness of the previous May, he decided to leave Ars secretly, assuming his bishop would not object to such action. He set out at one o'clock in the morning but was overtaken by John Pertinand. Together they proceeded to the home of Father Vianney's brother Francis, in Dardilly.

Catherine Lassagne later revealed that the Curé had confided his intention to leave Ars to her, and explained his motives:

"He planned to stay at his brother's house in a room prepared for him at his request, perhaps until such time as he could go elsewhere.... But he had said that if he could only be freed of the heavy burden of his parish, he wanted only to pray, do penance, and say Mass. He bemoaned his spiritual wretchedness, thought he was unworthy and unable to carry out the functions of a pastor. This caused him great sadness and... continued almost the whole time he remained at Ars, because I remember that he had been here scarcely two years when he was already thinking of leaving."

It is evident that this was one of his obsessions, and he had gotten it directly from his Fathers of the Desert.

Father Vianney's first flight ended rather quickly. Father Raymond went to him with the bishop's answer. The Curé of Ars was offered the choice of any parish or chapel he pleased, but the bishop would not let him leave the diocese.

Meanwhile the parishioners of Ars were in great desolation, offering prayers for their pastor's return. To their delight, he did come back to them. The village mayor, Count Prosper des Garets, welcomed him effusively:

"*Monsieur le Curé*, it was time you came back. I lost a great deal of sleep over it!" Many of the other parishioners could have said as much.

The Flight of 1853

Ten years later the same events were repeated. Again, the Curé of Ars was motivated by his desire to devote himself completely to his God. According to Catherine Lassagne, "his desire for solitude grew more and more imperative." The implication was that he had never given up this desire.

Once again he presumed he would have his bishop's permission. So sure was he of this that he made very explicit plans. Years before at the Seminary *Saint-Irénée* in Lyons, he had known Father Colin, who later founded the Marists. Father Colin had established a house of solitude and contemplation for those of his religious who might have the vocation for it. The house was located at La Neylière, not far from Saint-Symphorien-sur-Coise, about 45 kilometers (30 miles) from Lyons. Perpetual silence was the rule at this new version of a Trappist monastery. The community, formed on May 16, 1852, had seven priests and five lay brothers.

When Father Vianney heard about the new house of solitude, he was soon filled with the thought of going there to "weep over his poor life," as he was always saying. While Father Colin advised him not to do anything in haste, he had a cell prepared for his use in the event he actually did go to the house of solitude.

When Father Vianney finally tried to carry out his plan, he never got beyond the bridge over the Fontblin River at Ars. Although he again set out in the middle of the night, the alert was quickly sounded. This time, Father Toccanier, a diocesan missionary, was the curate assisting the pastor of Ars in his many duties. He held him firmly and spoke to him of Bishop Devie's command not to leave his post. He reminded him that he was under greater obligation than ever to respect his wishes. Besides, he saw to it that the road out of Ars was closed off by all the people who had been waiting in the church to go to confession. In this way, he gained time to implore the fleeing priest in the name of his beloved saints:

"How is it that you, *Monsieur le Curé*, who know the *Lives of the Saints* by heart, can forget the zeal of St. Martin who cried out when he already had his hand on his eternal reward: 'I do not refuse to work!' And you want to quit the battlefield! And what about the example of St. Philip Neri? Did he not say that when he reached the threshold of heaven, if a sinner came to request his ministry he would gladly leave the heavenly court to listen to him? And you, *Monsieur le Curé*, you dare to leave without hearing the confessions of these men and women who have come so far to see you?"

This plea, supported by the supplications of the crowd, won out over Father Vianney's yearning for solitude. He realized that his desire could be one of the Devil's tricks to drive him away from his apostolate under the pretext of seeking a loftier state of perfection. Humbly, he acknowledged:

"I have acted childishly!"

The point to remember in all this, as we have said, is that the principal wellspring of his spirituality was indeed the example of the Fathers of the Desert who had always haunted his thoughts since his boyhood, and whose great witness to the love of God-Trinity he had resolved to emulate.

Another Aspect of the Curé s Spirituality

We must take care not to distort the picture. Father Vianney was never a man of theory. He was no archaeologist in love with history who wanted to live in the past. True, he was permeated, so to speak, with the way of life of the Fathers of the Desert. He envied their holy courage, he walked boldly in their footsteps. But he was also a man of his own time, refusing to cast aside any of the riches of the Church available in the nineteenth century.

On the spiritual foundation drawn from the *Sayings of the Fathers,* bristling with austerities from another age, he erected a second spiritual structure born of his priestly formation in the seminary and centered on the Holy Eucharist.

So two spiritualities were wonderfully fused in John Mary Vianney's life: one ancient and the other modern. The latter originated at Saint Sulpice, which was an extension of the French School of Bérulle. It is true that he did not use the vocabulary of Bérulle, and was not trained directly by the Sulpicians at the Seminary *Saint-Irénée*. However, the diocesan priests who did train him were themselves formed in the Sulpician spirituality. This spirituality, according to the great 17th-century ideal, had supreme reverence for Jesus, the eternal Priest, the one perfect Adorer of his Father in the Eucharist. It was characterized by a profound love for the divine Savior, great concern for everything relating to the celebration of the Eucharistic liturgy and adoration of the Blessed Sacrament. All these elements were guiding forces in the spiritual life of the Curé of Ars.

It can be said that the real presence of Jesus in the Blessed Sacrament was at the very heart of his devotion. Toward the end of his life, at least after 1847, he could sense the reality of this presence so keenly that the very thought of being close to the tabernacle filled him with tremulous joy. He could not teach his catechism classes with his back to Jesus Eucharistically present in the church, or even when he stood too close to the altar. That is why he set up a little pulpit on the side which came to be called "the catechism pulpit." It was not for his own personal comfort that he made this change, but out of his profound love and intense respect for the Eucharistic presence of Jesus in the tabernacle.

Magnificence of Divine Worship

Likewise, it was not out of a childish taste for pomp that he insisted from the start that nothing was ever beautiful enough for God. To his mind, the priestly vestments, the banners used in the processions, the canopy for the Blessed Sacrament should be more magnificent than the decorations of any human dwelling.

We have already spoken about the Feast of Corpus Christi, as it was celebrated at Ars. Father Vianney had succeeded in making it such a grandiose celebration that thousands of people thronged the unknown village of Ars to participate in it.

In his zeal to make divine worship as beautiful as possible, our saint was not acting as a sort of dilettante of religious art, as a poet who loved color and fanfare in religious ceremonies. It can truly be said he was guided by his supernatural faith, which attested to the primacy of the eternal and the invisible. It was truly a faith according to St. Paul's definition: "the confident assurance concerning what we hope for, and conviction about things we do not see" (Heb. 11:1). That is all that mattered to him. All else meant nothing.

In his immense desire for solitude and recollection, in his yearning for the life of a hermit far from the crowds, he thought he would still be able to celebrate the Eucharistic liturgy in a worthy manner.

Here we can see how the two wellsprings of his spirituality were joined as one. From the Fathers of the Desert he had gotten his love of solitude, silence, penance, and lofty contemplation, together with his scorn for the basic needs of the body such as food, rest, sleep, and reasonable comfort. From the Sulpician School he had his love for Jesus the Victim, the Holy Sacrifice of the Mass, the Blessed Sacrament, in a word for the Eucharist in its complementary aspects as sacrifice and sacrament.

Actually the two spiritualities are not in contradiction. They tend to intermingle very well. The waters from the two wellsprings flowed in a single stream in our saint's soul.

We might mention in passing that early in his ministry at Ars he revived the Confraternity of the Blessed Sacrament. At the time, it had only one surviving member from before the French Revolution, an old peasant known as *Père Chaffangeon*.

It was *Père Chaffangeon* who explained to a neighbor what he was doing when he stayed in church so long:

"I keep looking at Him, and He keeps looking at me!"

Father Vianney's love of the Holy Eucharist found expression in his encouragement of frequent Communion among the laity. We should remember that during that period of the Church's history in France even the best pastors seemed to be going too far when they permitted their parishioners to receive Holy Communion four times a year, and perhaps on feastdays. This shows us how far ahead of his time the Curé of Ars was. His supernatural insights surely made of him a precursor of St. Pius X, the great apostle of frequent Communion.

When the Curé of Ars established the Confraternity of the Rosary for the women, one of their duties was never to leave the Blessed Sacrament without an adorer. Thus a perpetual guard of honor was formed around the Blessed Sacrament. Among those who took part in it were Mlle. d'Ars, the widow Claudine Renard, Mlle. Lacand, Mlle. Pignault, Catherine Lassagne and the two other directors of La Providence.

The tabernacle became the very heart and soul of the parish, the center sending forth rays of light and warmth toward all the souls entrusted to the care of Father Vianney.

The Degrees of Prayer

Once again we must return to the fundamental theme of this short biography: prayer. It was through prayer that John Mary Vianney grew spiritually, and it is in the context of his progress in prayer that we must try to measure his ultimate holiness. As we

*The people of Ars loved celebrations, and First Communion
was an occasion of special joy for the Curé and his flock.*

have already said, it is the "perpetual fervor of his prayer and penance" that the Church invites us to venerate in him.

Let us briefly review the stages of his growth in prayer. He had learned to pray during his earliest childhood. As he later said: "I owe it to my mother. She was so wise!" As a child he used to pray instead of playing with the other children. If he disappeared from sight for a moment, he would be discovered praying in some quiet spot. He prayed in the fields where his sheep and cows grazed. He prayed as he tilled the soil around the vines with his older brother. He never stopped praying throughout his years as a student, that he might be intelligent enough to attain the priesthood. His prayer had already reached amazing heights at the time of his ordinations to the subdiaconate, the diaconate, and finally to the priesthood. From that time onward, his breviary and the Eucharistic liturgy offered him opportunities for the loftiest prayer.

On his way to the summits of prayer he had learned to meditate and progress in mental prayer. But, as we know, there are many degrees even in mental prayer. He had to start out like everyone else with discursive prayer, focussing his mind on an appropriate subject. Gradually he turned to contemplation in which the soul remains silent and lets God speak, or lets God act while surrendering itself completely to His action within it. In this stage the soul limits itself to the "loving, peaceful, and joyous attention to God's presence" about which St. John of the Cross writes.

But why cite St. John of the Cross when we can quote directly from Father Vianney? In one of his famous catechisms, he spoke of prayer in this way:

"The more we pray, the more we want to pray.... It is like a fish swimming first at the surface of the water, and then diving deeper but always moving ahead. The soul plunges, goes to great depths, and is lost in the delights of conversation with God."

Obviously he was speaking from personal experience and telling about his own life. The more he prayed, the more he wanted to pray. He had first learned vocal prayer, then mental prayer in discursive meditation. That was like the fish swimming at the surface. Later he "plunged" into God. He buried himself in the divine abyss, he lost himself "in the delights of conversation with God." In terms of mystical doctrine, this means that he knew and practiced the prayer of simplicity, the prayer of recollection, the prayer of union. For him prayer was far less a special spiritual exercise included in his daily program than a continual communion with God. This total immersion in prayer has been practiced by all the mystics, by the apostles, the martyrs, the confessors, the virgins, the Fathers of the Desert, the Fathers of the Church, the monks of all the religious Orders, in a word by all the saints before mental prayer became a formal spiritual exercise in the fifteenth and sixteenth centuries.

A question immediately arises in our minds. How, amid the continual inrush of penitents and pilgrims to Ars, could he possibly preserve his union with God? This is what we can truthfully call "the miracle of his life." We like to call it his secret of "rooting his action in contemplation."

Here is the way he expressed his aspirations:

"Oh! I wish I could lose myself and never find myself again except in God!"

He spoke these words to Mr. Gardette, who so testified at the beatification process.

Another witness, Hippolyte Pages, declared:

"He had acquired the habit of coming away from God in order to act when he had to, and returning to God through prayer as soon as he could."

Brother Jerome, who was his close associate at Ars, said:

"When the influx of pilgrims was so great that it prevented him from engaging in prolonged mental prayer, *Monsieur le Curé* made it a habit to choose a subject for meditation each morning to which he would relate all the actions of that day."

Our saint also spoke these revealing words to Father Dufour, concerning his mental prayer:

"I don't have time for mental prayer as a regular thing, but from the beginning of the day I try to unite myself very closely to our Lord, and then I act with this union in mind."

Thus, his whole life became a prayer of union. He was immersed in divine love, and could truthfully say with his customary simplicity:

"I have chosen the love of God as my portion."

John Mary Vianney did indeed attain the highest possible degree of prayer. The profound words of St. John of the Cross can be applied to him:

"O night that has joined
The Lover with his beloved,
The beloved transformed into her Beloved!"

The beloved is the mystical soul. The night is total loss of self in God. The union of the beloved with her Lover who is God is necessarily a transforming union. In fact, it is the union that both St. Teresa of Avila and St. John of the Cross have called spiritual marriage. This is the highest level to which a soul can attain on this earth. St. John Mary Vianney experienced this state, which he described in a charming way: "In the soul united to God, it is always springtime!"

Lofty Spiritual Favors

There can be no doubt, therefore, that the Curé of Ars personally experienced the loftiest spiritual favors recorded in the lives of the saints. He loved to talk about these favors in other saints, but has left us only a few fleeting glimpses of them in his own life. For he practiced with all his might the precept: "It is a good thing to hide the secret of the King."

Even so, almost without his realizing it he made some admissions which reveal a little of his hidden prayer life.

One day, he arrived at *La Providence*, his face radiant and transfigured.

"What a great favor!" he exclaimed in the presence of Catherine Lassagne. "What happiness, what an extraordinary happening!"

"What was it?" she asked.

"Over at the church! At the church!" he said simply as though regretting he had already said too much.

Another day, when he was eating his frugal meal at *La Providence* standing in front of a buffet that served him as a table, he talked to himself, thinking he was alone. Jeanne Marie Chanay happened to come in unnoticed, and heard him say with a sigh:

"After all, I haven't seen the Lord since last Sunday!"

"So you used to see him before Sunday?" she asked.

Taken by surprise, he turned around and said nothing more.

His Mass

Everyone who attended one of his Masses agreed that something extraordinary happened then between him and his divine Master. This is not to imply that he prolonged the Eucharistic liturgy beyond the appointed time. No one could claim he had ecstasies during his Masses. But anyone who really understands what kind of a man he was must assume that he had personally experienced what he described in one of his catechism classes in or about the year 1850:

"Here is the point. We are all earthly and our faith only shows us objects from a distance of three hundred leagues, as if God were on the other side of the sea. If we had a lively faith, we would certainly be able to see Him in the Blessed Sacrament. There are priests who see Him every day during the Holy Sacrifice of the Mass."

He often came away from saying Mass with a look of radiant happiness. Catherine Lassagne has related:

"When I saw him with that look of extraordinary happiness, I used to say to Brother Jerome: '*Monsieur le Curé* is certainly filled with great love of God today!'"

And yet, like all great spiritual men, he distrusted "consolations" because he considered them to be self-centered reactions.

"When we have no consolations, we serve God for God's own sake. When we have them, we are in danger of serving Him for ourselves."

Apparitions

We mention some of the apparitions that were granted to him, not to imply that these extraordinary happenings had anything to do with his holiness, but simply to give a complete account of his life. Some of the greatest saints never mentioned having had apparitions. He never did either. But God permitted that his secret should be revealed.

On May 8, 1840, a lady came to see him, Mlle. Etienette Durié. She was bringing a considerable sum of money intended for the parish missions which were very dear to our saint's heart. When she arrived, Father Vianney was alone in his room in the rectory. She went upstairs quietly and heard a dialogue between Father Vianney and a lady speaking in a gentle voice:

"What are you asking?" the voice said.

"Good Mother," said the Curé, "I ask for the conversion of sinners, the consolation of the afflicted, the relief of the sick, especially a lady who has long been suffering and is begging either to die or to be cured."

"She will get well," the voice answered. "But later on!"

As it happened the visitor was suffering from cancer. She was convinced that the sick person in question was herself. And so she rushed in through the half-open door. What did she see? Here is how she described the scene.

"Standing in front of the fireplace was a lady of medium height resplendent in her white dress on which were golden roses. Her slippers seemed to be white as snow. On her hands shone the richest diamonds. Her forehead was surrounded with a crown of stars that shone like the sun. I was dazzled.

"'Good Mother,' I said to her without waiting. 'Please take me to heaven!'

"'Later on.'

"'It's time, now, Mother!'

"'You will always be my child, and I shall always be your Mother!'"

Then the apparition vanished. The visitor had just received a great favor from heaven. For the Blessed Virgin Mary had appeared and spoken to her. For a moment, she was beside herself as a result of what had just happened to her.

Her testimony continues:

"When I had regained my senses, I noticed *Monsieur le Curé* standing in front of his table, his hands joined on his breast, his face radiant, his eyes motionless. I almost feared he might be dead. Coming close to him, I pulled at a fold in his cassock.

"'O my God!' he said, 'Is it You?'

"'No, Father, it is I....'

"As I said these words, he came to himself and moved.

"'Where were you, Father? What have you just seen?'

"'I saw a lady.'

"'And I did too,' I answered. 'Who is this lady?'

"'If you say anything about it,' Father Vianney replied in a stern tone, 'you will never enter my house again.'

"'Should I tell you, Father, what I thought? I thought it was the Blessed Virgin.'

"'And you were not mistaken.... And so you saw her?'

"'Yes, I saw her and spoke to her. But now you must tell me what state you were in when I thought you were dead.'

"'Oh no! I was too happy to see my Mother!'

"'Good Father, it is certainly because of you that I saw her! When she comes back, consecrate me to her so that she may consecrate me to her divine Son!'

"The servant of God promised to do so, then he added:

"'You will get well....'

"'But when, Father?'

"'A little later on. Don't ask me so many questions.'

"Then, in a gentler tone, he added:

"'With the Blessed Virgin Mary and St. Philomena, we know each other very well.'"

Actually, Mlle. Etienette Durié was cured of cancer at Ars three and a half months later, on August 15, 1840.

The account we have just quoted was part of the testimony given at the beatification process. It can readily explain why the Curé of Ars once said to a distinguished visitor, pointing to a corner of his room:

"No one would dare set foot on that tile in the floor if he knew what happened there!"

Transformed by Love

The apparition we have just described certainly shows that the Curé of Ars was a close friend of the Lady who, in his own words, had been his first love. Even so, we must remember that the Church does not grant the honors of beatification and canonization simply on the basis of such heavenly favors.

What ranks first in importance is the degree of charity a person attains, and what we have called transforming union.

In order to understand what we are trying to say here, it is enough to reread the thirteenth chapter of St. Paul's first epistle to the Corinthians:

"If I speak with human tongues and angelic as well, but do not have love, I am a noisy gong, a clanging cymbal. If I have the gift of prophecy and, with full knowledge, comprehend all mysteries, if I have faith great enough to move mountains, but have not love, I am nothing. If I give everything I have to feed the poor and hand over my body to be burned, but have not love, I gain nothing" (1 Cor. 13:1-3).

Admittedly, the Apostle separates in his thinking some things that are scarcely separable. What he is trying to say is that nothing has any value before God except through the charity it expresses.

In the eyes of God, the Curé of Ars' visions, his outstanding gift of reading the consciences of others and even of foretelling the future, even his prodigious charitable activities and unbelievable austerities — all these things would have had no value at all without charity.

That is why the transforming love that we believe we have shown in him is the most important aspect of his life.

Another Jesus Christ

Father John Mary Vianney still had to prove that he truly conformed to the perfect ideal of his dignity as a priest.

As we conclude our study of his spiritual life, we are led to the conclusion that he did indeed live up to this ideal.

What are the essential marks of the soul of our Lord Jesus Christ?

Two loves fused as one—love of His Father and love of His brothers—filled His soul, explained His whole life, all His actions, from the smallest to the greatest. From the moment He appeared in this world His only thought was to do the will of His Father. And this will is our salvation and sanctification.

This is the entire message of the Gospel. Christ's miracles, His early hidden life and His public life, His Passion and death, and then His Resurrection and Ascension—all these were for our sakes as well as for His Father. Throughout the life of Christ, the glory of God coincided in every instance with our eternal happiness.

Transforming love in a saint, especially if this saint is a priest, must be revealed under this two-fold aspect: a total dedication to the will of God combined with an unbounded love for souls.

Now, what do we find in the life of the Curé of Ars?

It can truly be said that he lived, breathed, and worked only to love God and to bring others to love Him. That is all he ever wanted, and he wanted it with all his being, with all his might. No one could cite anything he ever said that would have implied anything else or revealed any other desire on his part.

He came to resemble our Lord Jesus Christ as closely as his nature allowed. Though he was not richly endowed with talents, he gave everything he had to God like the poor widow who offered all her meager savings to the Temple of Jerusalem. He surrendered himself into the hands of God, and God made it eminently apparent that He could do wonderful things even with such a defective instrument. He chose to take John Mary Vianney's limited intellect and pour His divine light into it. He accepted his earnest desire to serve, strengthening his will, and warming it in His divine love. And thus God took a simple man wholeheartedly at His service, and raised him to the loftiest heights of love to which any human being can reach.

It was because the Curé of Ars was well aware of the immense work God's grace had accomplished within him that he could truthfully say:

"The love of God is my life work."

The Missions

There is undeniable evidence of Father Vianney's great love for souls in the convict's life he lived for their sakes. For he was truly a prisoner by his own choice, a prisoner in the confessional fifteen to sixteen hours a day.

Priests who hear confessions know what this means — a continuous effort to listen, to be patient, gentle, kind, and understanding, hour after hour. This demands a great love of souls.

Those of our readers who do not know the fatigue involved in hearing confessions can take the word of those of us who have learned from experience what a heavy cross this priestly labor can be.

We say that Jesus was crucified for the sake of souls. In a sense we can say that Father Vianney was crucified by sinful souls. That is why he said toward the end of his life: "Oh! The sinners will finally kill the poor sinner!"

We should mention another way in which Father Vianney showed his concern for the spiritual welfare of the faithful. He would have wanted to convert all the parishes of France at once. His zeal was not restricted to his own village of Ars, but grew with the ever-growing pilgrimages. One of the inevitable results of these pilgrimages was that many of the visitors to Ars began to offer him gifts for his various charitable projects. We have already spoken of *La Providence,* the girls' school he founded, and of his efforts to make divine worship as splendid as possible, especially for the Feast of Corpus Christi.

In addition, he had the greatest concern about the need for periodic parish missions. Every parish, he knew, needed some sort of religious renewal from time to time, and this was usually accomplished by means of parish missions held every ten years or so.

And so our saint began to save money in order to finance the greatest possible number of parish missions every ten years. He even became "a miser for God" to this end. He went about his "hoarding" in this way. He calculated that 3,000 francs at 5% interest brought in 150 francs. At the end of ten years this amounted to 1,500 francs, which was ample to cover the expenses of a mission. Therefore, 3,000 francs would provide a parish with a mission every ten years in perpetuity.

And so Father Vianney started acquiring funds in amounts of 3,000 francs. When someone came to ask advice he would speak of his missions, mentioning the amount of 3,000 francs. He obtained unbelievable results. For instance, one lady told him she had decided to give him 50 francs for his charitable works. When he explained to her the importance of the parish missions, she decided to send him

6,000 francs so that he might found two perpetual missions through her help.

When money came in to establish a new mission, Father Vianney would be exuberant.

One morning he said to Brother Athanasius in the sacristy:

"Brother, did you get up early this morning?"

"The same as usual," the Brother answered.

"That's too bad! If you had imitated me you would have had a wonderful day. I have been given money for a mission, and there is even some money left over.... As I was coming out of the rectory during the night, I met a young man who had been waiting for me and who gave me 1,000 francs for this work. Then someone else in the Chapel of St. John the Baptist gave me the same amount. Finally a third person arrived who completed the sum, and gave even more."

The Brother added, as he told the incident, "And it was only seven o'clock in the morning when *Monsieur le Curé* told me this story."

The Mass that he celebrated that morning must have been one of great thanksgiving.

On another occasion in July, 1855, Father Vianney went to visit the missionary priests of Pont-d'Ains, who had a residence in Ars. One of these missioners, Father Monnin, who would later write his biography, exclaimed when he saw him:

"*Monsieur le Curé*, how happy you look today!"

"I should think so! This morning I discovered that I had 200,000 francs" [this would amount to many millions of francs in present-day money].

"And this capital has been deposited in the most solid bank in the world. I lent it to the three richest persons anywhere in the world."

"And who are these three persons?"

"The Persons of the Blessed Trinity."

The Canon's Mozzetta [1]

In connection with Father Vianney's financial ventures we can mention the episode of his appointment as Canon of Belley.

It was not customary to confer the title of canon on the pastor of such a tiny place as Ars. But Ars was no longer an unknown rural parish. Bishop Chalandon, the successor to Bishop Devie, decided to demonstrate his respect for the humble pastor of Ars by bringing the canon's mozzetta to him personally. He thought it best not to forewarn him of his coming, lest he try to refuse the honor.

And so on Monday, October 25, 1852, the bishop came to Ars, accompanied by a vicar general. When Father Vianney was informed of his coming as he sat in his confessional, he hastened to come out and offer the prelate holy water according to the ceremonial of the time. Suddenly the bishop brought out an object from beneath his own mozzetta. The Curé of Ars understood. The bishop wanted to make him a canon. He protested, he begged, but all in vain. The mozzetta was draped over his shoulders, and lay askew over his surplice.

He returned to the church looking like a condemned man. But after the bishop had gone and he had overcome his own excitement, he figured that he could increase the capital he needed for his beloved parish missions by simply selling the canon's mozzetta he had just received.

One generous person offered him 50 francs. He did not fail to inform his bishop of the transaction in a respectful letter. Afterward he was often heard to say:

"Oh! If only His Excellency will give me another, then I'll make some money out of it."

---

1. A mozzetta is a short cape with a small ornamental hood worn by the Pope and privileged dignitaries, including canons.

The Legion of Honor

Three years later, at the request of the Sub-prefect of Trévoux, Father Vianney was decorated with the Legion of Honor, something unheard-of for an insignificant country pastor like him. This time he did not have the consolation of having something to sell for his missions. He never wore his *Croix d'Honneur* during his life, but it was placed on his coffin after his death.

One day, he said: "If I could sell myself in order to give something to the Blessed Virgin Mary I'd certainly do it!" Such was his "miserliness for the sake of God."

The Parish Missions

In closing we might mention that before he died he had established missions in perpetuity in over 100 parishes. This represented a capital of 300,000 francs wisely invested in "the bank of the Blessed Trinity."

It is now time for us to tell about Father John Mary Vianney's departure for the bank he loved so much.

The Last Years - Death Comes - Posthumous Glory in the Church

Last Endeavors

According to Catherine Lassagne, "After his last attempt to flee — in 1853 — our holy *Curé* hardly spoke at all of going away, except perhaps departing from the present life into eternity. He often said: 'We are going away. We'll have to die and soon!' He seemed to have the thought of death continually before him. His health was failing rapidly. Even so, he curtailed none of his labors or vigils. For several years he had continued to hear confessions in winter until seven o'clock in the evening, and in summer until a later hour. He never wasted a moment."

This is certainly the picture of a man devoting himself with ever greater zeal to his terrible task, and becoming increasingly weary and exhausted. Testimonies about that period of his life prove that the pilgrimage to Ars had not declined but on the contrary continued to grow from year to year. It was after 1853 that the number of pilgrims reached a total of 100,000 a year and even more. This means that presumably 260 pilgrims arrived each day, swelling the number of daily confessions to be heard by the Curé of Ars.

His rule of life remained the same as it had always been. However, it now became harder for him to rouse himself from his short rest which was often interrupted by exhausting fits of coughing. At one o'clock in the morning he continued to make the same heroic effort that he had always made. He would rise and drag himself to his church and his confessional.

Final Joys

One of Father Vianney's last joys, after his second flight from Ars, was the proclamation of the dogma of the Immaculate Conception on December 8, 1854. He had always had fervent devotion to the Blessed Virgin Mary, immaculately conceived. On this occasion he had a magnificent vestment made for use at the Mass. It was embroidered in gold on a background of blue velvet, and was approved by the bishop in spite of its unliturgical color.

Exhausted as he was, the Curé of Ars insisted on celebrating the High Mass on December 8, 1854, proudly wearing his new vestment.

He was also happy to be able to preach a mission in his own parish at the end of the year 1858. This time, he was too weak to accompany the missioners on visits to the families of the parish. He apologized for not going with them in a touching letter in which he bade farewell to everyone. It read in part:

"The other times, I was the one who went to see you: you never refused me anything. I thank you.... Today it is the missionary who visits you, but it is as if I came. I accompany him with my heart.... Alas! There are still sinners in the parish. I must go away so that another can convert them."

In any event, the thought of his approaching death did not keep him from making grandiose plans.

It was toward the end of this period, late in 1858, that he asked the architect, Bossan of Lyons, to make plans for a "beautiful church" that he intended to dedicate to St. Philomena. He visualized a large and magnificent structure. On April 2, 1859, he began a campaign for pledges, and set himself down for 1,000 francs. These plans were carried out after his death and can be seen in the beautiful basilica of Ars as it exists today.

Forebodings

The Curé of Ars seems to have had presentiments of his approaching death. Before the Feast of Corpus Christi in 1858 he had been given a beautiful ribbon. Catherine Lassagne had said to him: "*Monsieur le Curé*, this will be useful to you for the Corpus Christi procession, to help you hold up the monstrance."

"He answered me with a smile: 'I shall not carry the Blessed Sacrament twice.'"

Father Vianney did carry the monstrance in the Corpus Christi procession of 1858. However, in 1859 he was so weakened that he could not. The monstrance had to be handed to him at each of the repositories so that he could hold it up in benediction.

That same year, when he sent Catherine Lassagne to the town of Cibeins to collect a small annuity that had been willed to him, he said to her: "This will be the last time I collect that annuity." After a moment's pause, he repeated in a more confident tone: "Yes, that will be the last time."

According to Catherine Lassagne, "He had periodically suffered from an exhausting cough. It would abate for a while and then return. But in the year 1859 this cough became so stubborn that no remedy could cure it. It was pitiful to hear him. When he had a coughing spell in the confessional, he had to stop. One day he apologized for the time he wasted coughing.

Some witnesses have said that this cough sounded like heart-rending cries and sobs welling up in his throat. We have an account of it written by a contemporary journalist, George Seigneur. This report was dated August 20, 1859, sixteen days after our saint's death, and gives us a picture of Ars at that time.

"Last March I was following the road from Villefranche. It was thronged with pilgrims. Some were going to Ars, others were coming back.... I shall never forget the simple and solemn sight at the entrance of the village.

"The pilgrims who couldn't get into the church were standing at the door, in the cemetery, in the surrounding alleys, waiting their turn. There were pictures of the Curé of Ars everywhere, teaching catechism to the children, visiting the sick, and so on. They peered out of the store windows, and could be seen among the rosaries, medals, holy candles, etc....

"It was four o'clock in the afternoon when I entered the church. The Curé of Ars was in the confessional. I had just knelt down when I heard a sob that I cannot describe. It came from the confessional. Was it a cry of suffering? Was it a cry of love? Every ten minutes or so the sob would be heard again. It heaved from the Curé of Ars' choking lungs as he strove to overcome his exhaustion. But the cry of suffering became a cry of love as if it were the effort of a soul chained to earth seeking to find a passage to heaven.

"The Curé of Ars had been there since two o'clock in the morning, alternating the confessions of the men, women, and children. Since two o'clock in the morning he had interrupted his confessions only twice. The first time was in order to say Mass. The second was to give an instruction from the pulpit, to eat his only meal which consisted of soup, and to rest ten minutes or perhaps a quarter of an hour while he chatted. In a few moments he returned to celebrate Benediction, gave a second instruction at the foot of the altar, heard confessions until nine o'clock in the evening, returning to his rectory to say his own prayers, then go to bed at eleven o'clock or midnight, only to get up again at one o'clock in the morning. That was the life he lived every day and every night.

"Around five o'clock in the evening, there was a ripple in the crowd. I saw an old man come out of the confessional, wearing a torn cassock and a plain surplice. He was very thin. His face was perfectly heart-shaped, narrow and tapering from the cheeks down to the chin, and with a very broad forehead. His whole face was illumined by his large eyes that shone like two diamonds, his white hair looked like a flaxen diadem. Instead of making a way for him the people crowded against him to touch his surplice, his cassock, his hair, his emaciated hands.

"He often staggered under the crowd's pressure, and I feared for a moment he would fall. He allowed himself to be pushed around, opening a path for himself gently, humbly, without shoving anyone back...."

As we read these lines, are we not reminded of Jesus Christ surrounded and pressed by the crowds and giving Himself to everyone?

Our journalist, George Seigneur, was also struck by the similarity, for he went on to say:

"That evening I had a talk with him.... A supernatural radiance seemed to emanate from his soul, his face, his glance. I can still see him, leaning on the sacristy table, and I can remember how frighteningly he resembled the picture of our Lord which hung on the wall. It was a stark picture of the Redeemer after His scourging, with the flesh of

His back torn to shreds as if it were a veil, making the bones visible. The Savior's face was turned to one side, toward the spectator, as if to remind him that the prophet's words had been fulfilled to the letter: They counted my bones...."

In the last chapter we concluded our discussion of our saint's spirituality by speaking about his transforming union with God. Interestingly enough, George Seigneur reached the same conclusion by a very different path. He wrote:

"By dint of imitating his Master, the Curé of Ars came to resemble Him. Suffering and joy were fused within him. His forehead and cheeks, furrowed with wrinkles, sometimes grew dark and seemed to sag under the weight of invisible sufferings. All of a sudden he would raise his head, his face would light up, his wrinkles would change into rays of light, his transfigured flesh became transparent like the flesh of a child, his eyes were aflame with a heavenly fire....

"That's exactly the way I saw him, both in public and in private, reproducing the tortures and the glories of the Word Incarnate, receiving and bearing by turn as in a fiery mirror the gloom of Calvary and the splendor of Tabor...."

The End Approaches

The summer of 1859 was especially hot and unbearable. In the Dombes area of France the atmosphere was very heavy, oppressive and as though on fire. That did not keep the pilgrims from coming to Ars in ever-growing numbers. It was as if they understood the Curé would soon be snatched away from them.

By now Father Vianney's strength was dwindling from day to day. His voice was almost inaudible. Even those in the first rows of the church could not hear him when he gave his daily instruction.

The Curé's rectory grounds, thronged with pilgrims.

He no longer talked about taking time to "weep over his poor life." One day, he even said to Catherine Lassagne:

"If a priest were to die because of the hardships and labors he endured for the glory of God and the salvation of souls, that wouldn't be a bad thing."

Catherine commented: "From his air of contentment, he seemed to desire such a death."

As far as he was concerned, he was no longer looking forward to the peaceful death of the hermit, but to the painful death of the martyrs.

John Mary Vianney wanted to die in the line of duty. Indeed the day came when he was so totally exhausted and tortured by his incessant cough, overcome by the heat and overwhelmed by the burden of hearing confessions that he felt he had to go out of the church to breathe some fresh air and to rest in his courtyard. Catherine tells us about it:

"That night he returned home with Brother Jerome. I came to see if he wanted something to eat. The sun had set, he was very, very tired....

"We both retired and left him alone, not without some anxiety. Then, around one o'clock after midnight he knocked to summon someone. I arrived first and asked him how he was. He answered:

"'This is the end of my poor life! You must go and get *Monsieur le Curé* of Jassans.'" That was his confessor.

Soon afterwards, he said again to Brother Jerome: "This is the end of my poor life!"

The next morning the pastor of Jassans and the physician were summoned. The latter stated:

"If the heat wave subsides, we can hope for the best. But if it continues we shall lose him."

As it happened the heat wave continued. Father Vianney could speak now only in a whisper. When he was offered the last sacraments he wanted to receive them at once.

His Last Communion

John Mary Vianney's last Communion was a very tearful one. As Catherine Lassagne recalls it:

"His faith in our Lord was very strong. Even before anyone arrived in his room with the Blessed Sacrament, he was filled with great emotion and tears flowed from his eyes. Brother Jerome asked him the reason for his tears, and he answered:

"'Ah. When I think I am about to receive the Lord for the last time!'"

But what touched him most of all was the thought of God's kindness. In a low whisper, he murmured:

"How good God is! When we cannot go and see Him, He comes to us!"

The ringing of the church bell had summoned the faithful. The dying man's confessor, preceded by about twenty priests who had flocked in from the surrounding area, was bringing the saint his last Holy Communion.

After receiving the sacred host in an atmosphere of deep emotion, he was given the sacrament of Extreme Unction, now known as the Anointing of the Sick.

The oppressive heat continued to cause the dying priest great discomfort.

During the evening of August 3rd, Bishop de Langalerie of Belley hastened to the side of the Curé of Ars. After his visit, the bishop went over to the church and asked the crowd to pray for the dying man.

Death Comes

It seemed to all who witnessed our saint's last hours on earth that he was continually in the presence of God. His missioners were with him, watching through the night. About ten o'clock in the evening on August 3rd, it looked as though the end was imminent. Father Toccanier gave him the plenary indulgence for the dying.

John Mary Vianney's last agony had begun. At midnight Father Monnin gave him his crucifix to kiss, and slowly recited the liturgical prayers for the dying, pausing between the prayers in deep silence.

He had come to the words:

"May God's holy angels come to meet him and bring him into the heavenly Jerusalem."

Precisely at that moment, Christ's faithful worker, having completed his task, fell asleep in the Lord, gently, effortlessly, without a struggle.

It was two o'clock in the morning, August 4, 1859. Just then a thunderstorm broke over the village of Ars, filling the night with thunderclaps and streaks of lightning.

Our holy priest had reached the age of seventy-three years, two months, twenty-seven days. He had been the pastor of Ars for forty-one years, five months, and twenty-three days.

A Triumphant Funeral

The news of Father John Mary Vianney's death was transmitted by telegraph to every part of France. Immediately, all the neighboring villages stirred into action. The pastors hastened to come with their parishioners to render supreme homage to the man everyone already considered to be a saint. Church bells tolled not only at Ars but in all the churches in the surrounding area.

For two days the crowds filed past his mortal remains. His face was clothed in the great calm and majesty that only death confers.

The local stores were raised for souvenirs. Pictures, rosaries, crucifixes, and other objects were touched to his body by two Brothers and two students from the public school. Even the elder trees in the little courtyard of the rectory were stripped of their leaves.

So many strangers thronged the village of Ars that there was not enough food to go around. Besides, for lack of accommodations many had to spend the night out under the stars.

The funeral was held on August 6th, at eight o'clock in the morning. It has been estimated that about 6,000 of the faithful attended the triumphal ceremony which was presided over by the Bishop of Belley assisted by 300 priests.

The funeral cortege left the rectory and proceeded through the streets of the village, coming to a halt on the square behind the church. The body was placed in front of the calvary in the center of the square. Bishop de Langalerie then gave a eulogy that had many weeping. He opened with a commentary on Christ's words:

"Well done! You are an industrious and reliable servant.... Come, share your master's joy!" (Mt. 25:21).

Looking out on the silent throng, the prelate said:

"How many years, how many centuries perhaps has it been since we have seen a priestly life unfold under similar conditions, so fruitfully, with such great sanctity, a life continuously under attack, spent and consumed in God's service!... There is no way to replace a Curé of Ars!... The whole of France has lost a priest who did her honor and whom people came to visit and consult from all of her provinces...."

Then the religious ceremony continued in the church, in the presence only of the local authorities, the clergy, and members of Father Vianney's family. But a religious silence hovered over the entire village. The throng outside the church knelt or stood up by turns as the church bells tolled.

It was not until August 14th that the Curé of Ars' body was buried in a niche dug at the center of his church. His remains were to stay there until 1904, when they were placed in the reliquary where pilgrims venerate it to this day.

Glorification of John Mary Vianney

A stream of visitors began to come to our saint's tomb. The pilgrimage of Ars was continuing in a new form. People no longer came to the Curé of Ars to confess their sins. Now they came to pray to him as one of God's servants, as an intercessor for them before God. There was such a spontaneous tendency to venerate the relics of the Curé of Ars that steps had to be taken to put a stop to it. It was necessary to prevent any anticipation of the Church's decisions as to his sanctity, for only the Church has the responsibility and the right to proclaim that anyone is a saint.

The beatification process began as early as 1862. It required 200 sessions, and closed in 1865. An authentic copy of the proceedings covering 1,674 in-folio pages had been taken to the tribunal of Rome, where the decree of beatification was proclaimed on April 17, 1904. There had been no dearth of miracles to support the beatification of John Mary Vianney. In fact, seventeen could have been presented. However, the advocate of the cause chose only two, as required. The beatification ceremony took place at St. Peter's Basilica in Rome, on Sunday, January 8, 1905.

Two new miracles were recorded with a view to the canonization, which was celebrated on Pentecost, May 31, 1925, under the pontificate of Pope Pius XI.

Pius X, also a former country pastor, had beatified the Curé of Ars.

Conclusion and Prayer

As we come to the end of this little book, a twofold sentiment seems called for on our part: first, a sense of humility, and second, a great trust.

Humility: This is the sentiment that fills our hearts as we contemplate the courage and heroism of John Mary Vianney. We cannot help feeling very small and remiss in God's service, in the presence of this hero of divine love.

Trust: Since, as St. Paul says, love does not die, this saint who loved sinners so much will have pity on us. We can confidently address to him, with adaptations, the prayer that Catherine Lassagne placed at the end of her memoirs:

"Great nobleman of God, I dedicated to you this brief remembrance of your virtues, so that you may ask for me especially at the hour of death the protection of the Blessed Virgin Mary whom you loved so much. I beg you, do not forget me before the throne of God's mercy, you who reconciled so many sinners with God when you lived on this earth. Since charity is perfect in heaven, you will certainly practice it toward the author and all the readers of this little book, though it is imperfect and fails to measure up to your great merits!"

The celebration of the Curé's beatification in 1905.

St. Paul Book & Media Centers

ALASKA
750 West 5th Ave., Anchorage, AK 99501; 907-272-8183

CALIFORNIA
3908 Sepulveda Blvd., Culver City, CA 90230; 310-397-8676
5945 Balboa Ave., San Diego, CA 92111; 619-565-9181
46 Geary Street, San Francisco, CA 94108; 415-781-5180

FLORIDA
145 S.W. 107th Ave., Miami, FL 33174; 305-559-6715

HAWAII
1143 Bishop Street, Honolulu, HI 96813; 808-521-2731

ILLINOIS
172 North Michigan Ave., Chicago, IL 60601; 312-346-4228

LOUISIANA
4403 Veterans Memorial Blvd., Metairie, LA 70006; 504-887-7631

MASSACHUSETTS
50 St. Paul's Ave., Jamaica Plain, Boston, MA 02130; 617-522-8911
Rte. 1, 885 Providence Hwy., Dedham, MA 02026; 617-326-5385

MISSOURI
9804 Watson Rd., St. Louis, MO 63126; 314-965-3512

NEW JERSEY
561 U.S. Route 1, Wick Plaza, Edison, NJ 08817; 908-572-1200

NEW YORK
150 East 52nd Street, New York, NY 10022; 212-754-1110
78 Fort Place, Staten Island, NY 10301; 718-447-5071

OHIO
2105 Ontario Street, Cleveland, OH 44115; 216-621-9427

PENNSYLVANIA
510 Holstein Street, Bridgeport, PA 19405; 215-277-7728

SOUTH CAROLINA
243 King Street, Charleston, SC 29401; 803-577-0175

TENNESSEE
4811 Poplar Ave., Memphis, TN 38117; 901-761-0874

TEXAS
114 Main Plaza, San Antonio, TX 78205; 210-224-8101

VIRGINIA
1025 King Street, Alexandria, VA 22314; 703-549-3806

GUAM
285 Farenholt Avenue, Suite 308, Tamuning, Guam 96911; 671-646-7745

CANADA
3022 Dufferin Street, Toronto, Ontario, Canada M6B 3T5; 416-781-9131